FATAL FASCINATION

FATAL
FASCINATION

BY

NIGEL BALCHIN
C. S. FORESTER
ERIC LINKLATER
CHRISTOPHER SYKES

 LITTLE, BROWN AND COMPANY

BOSTON • TORONTO

12505

CONTENTS

NIGEL BALCHIN

Burnt Njal—
The Irredeemable Crime

THERE is a tablet on the walls of Rugby School to the memory of William Webb Ellis 'who, with a fine disregard of the rules of football as played in his time, first picked up the ball in his arms and ran with it, thus originating the distinctive feature of the Rugby game'.

No one would suggest that in inventing Rugby football William Webb Ellis committed a crime, yet after consulting half a dozen dictionaries and encyclopaedias I can find no better definition of a crime than 'a disregarding of the rules currently accepted'. The criminal is usually either a very dull person who has not the intelligence or ability to get what he wants by legal means or a psychopath who feels himself to be above the law. George Joseph Smith, the 'Brides in the Bath Murderer', made in all about five thousand pounds out of fifteen years of bigamy and murder, and relative to the risks he runs and the strains he must undergo, the average burglar must be one of the most poorly paid men in the country. At the opposite end of the social scale of crime, Hitler was responsible for the murder of millions of Jews. Yet all three are merely examples of a disregard of the rules currently accepted by some particular society or humanity in general.

But though the criminal is always a person who breaks the rules we certainly do not accept that everyone who breaks the rules is a criminal. These rules are constantly changing, and have been changing all through history, and the criminal of one century may easily be the hero of the next, and vice versa. Matthew Hopkins, the Witch Finder General, was something of a hero to many of the men of his own day, and he was

9

certainly a tool in the enforcement of the law of the day against witchcraft. Today we see him as a criminal. By contrast Richard Parker, who was hanged for his part in the naval mutiny at the Nore in 1797, was certainly a criminal according to the law of his day, but we see him now as a brave, if not particularly wise, rebel against the inhuman conditions which existed at that time in the Navy. Seventeen hundred and fifty years earlier a much greater social reformer had been crucified for his defiance of the currently accepted rules. 'We have a law, and by that law he ought to die.'

The rule-breaker may be anything between the excreta of society and its finest flower, but he is obviously always a *product* of society. A man alone upon a desert island can hardly commit a crime (except possibly by committing suicide). It is only when men come to live together in societies that rules of behaviour have to be made, and until there are rules there can be no crime.

But crime and the criminal are the products of society in another sense also. For any society produces not only certain laws, but a certain environment, and it is this environment which, whilst acceptable to most, turns certain men into criminals. It is fairly certain that crime is not hereditary, and that there never was such a person as a man 'born to be hanged'. The sociologists are always telling us that most of the blame for juvenile delinquency rests with parents. They have not provided a suitable environment and suitable control for their children. Parents might reply that exactly the same is true of adult delinquency. The parent—in this instance society—has failed to provide the suitable environment and the suitable controls.

*   *   *   *

The crime I want to consider occurred in Iceland just about a thousand years ago, when a noble-minded, generous, and wise old man, whom everybody respected, was burnt to death in his house with his wife and all his family. The crime was committed on the orders of another thoughtful, noble-hearted man, almost equally respected. I have chosen it for several reasons. It is a magnificent story, and, in the form which it has come down to us, magnificently told. The Norse Saga of Burnt Njal is by common consent the greatest and most perfect of all the Sagas. It is not only an account of a blood feud and the crimes which sprang from it, but an epic tragedy on the grandest scale, comparable with anything produced by the great Greek playwrights or by Shakespeare, and in some ways surpassing them. Most great tragedy has shown men in the grip of fate or of some supernatural or monstrous power. Men in Greek tragedy are the mere playthings of the gods. The plots of both *Hamlet* and *Macbeth* depend to some extent on the supernatural element. The tragedy of *Othello* springs from the monumental villainy of Iago—a man who has decided to say 'Evil, be thou my good'. The Saga of Burnt Njal does not use any of this apparatus. Capricious gods are not concerned. The supernatural hardly enters into the story, and there are no monumental villains. All the principal characters are men with many fine qualities of bravery and decency, and often of wisdom and foresight. They have failings, but they are very understandable ones. Yet the tragedy springs with absolute inevitability from the characters of these men and from the nature of the society in which they lived.

It is this last quality which is, to me, the most interesting aspect of the story of Burnt Njal. The tragedy is not only a very human and understandable one; it is also of high social significance, with an uncomfortably clear bearing on the state of the world today—our world seen through the wrong end of a telescope. At its end we do not say 'There but for the grace of God go I', but 'There but for the help of God will go mankind'.

THE BACKGROUND OF THE CRIME

In the year A.D. 872 Harald Fairhair finally brought the other Norwegian chiefs under his rule and founded the kingdom of

Norway. Rather than accept the King's supremacy many of the chiefs sailed away north and west to Scotland, Orkney, and eventually to Iceland, where land was freely available and each chief might be 'his own master, acknowledging no overlord'.

This Icelandic community was one of the most remarkable and interesting societies in history. The Icelanders were not just barbarians. They were able and brave, with a strong sense of humour and considerable good taste. Their womenfolk enjoyed a status not achieved by women in most parts of Europe until some hundreds of years later. They were magnificent seamen, and even reached America some five hundred years before Columbus.

They were not by any means lawless by nature. In fact, as we shall see later, they had almost too much interest in fine, cunning legal points, which sometimes remind us of Groucho Marx and A. Cheever Loophole, the Legal Eagle. If they were not very law-abiding it was mainly because there was not much law to abide by. The whole reason why they left Norway and founded the Icelandic community had been to escape any system of central government; and it was precisely this absence of any central government to make and enforce laws which was the fatal flaw in Iceland's social structure.

The nearest approach to a legislative and judicial system was the THING. There were a number of local THINGS which dealt with smaller local matters, but by far the most important was the ALTHING, which was an annual meeting of all the chiefs at which problems and complaints were raised and discussed. But whereas the ALTHING might discuss a dispute and give a ruling on it, it had no means of enforcing its decision, since it had no police force and no army, and any chief who felt himself strong enough to do so could simply defy it. The ALTHING, in fact, with its simultaneous attempt to maintain order and retain individual independence, had exactly the same problems and exactly the same weaknesses as the United Nations Organization has today. It was a gallant attempt to practise a sort of primitive half-democracy, and like all attempts to practise democracy, whether primitive or not, it left the way wide open for pressure groups, lobbying, and plain, straightforward power politics.

One of the common problems with which the ALTHING was called upon to deal was the blood feud. The Norsemen had no high view of the sanctity of human life, whether their own or any other man's. There was nothing disgraceful or dishonourable in killing your enemy, even if you caught him at a disadvantage. It is strange that the Norsemen, with their considerable sense of *noblesse oblige*, should have been so ready to lay murderous ambushes in which a dozen men would attack one. Presumably the principle was that a man, like a boxer in the ring, should be prepared to guard himself at all times. It was certainly no breach of the 'generally accepted rules' of conduct to kill an enemy, as long as the slaying was at once 'proclaimed'. In other words, it had to be made public and must not be done in secret.

Such a killing, however, automatically produced a blood feud. The dead man's next of kin inherited the blood feud just as they inherited his money and goods, and they then had various alternatives. To do nothing was an abiding disgrace which no family of honour could possibly accept. It could therefore either kill the killer—thereby continuing the feud— or it could accept a sum of money in atonement for the killing; or it could refer the whole matter to the ALTHING and ask for its ruling. No shame attached to accepting money in atonement for the murder of a relative. The main problem was to agree the right and proper sum, having regard to the dead man's rank and general standing in the community. Once this sum was agreed, either privately between the parties or as the result of a ruling of the ALTHING, the money would be paid over in the form of so many ounces of silver, and the matter, in theory at least, would be closed. It was not considered honourable to continue a quarrel once atonement had been accepted.

But this charmingly simple way of dealing with murder was

liable to break down in two fairly obvious ways. If the kinsman murdered was a close and much loved one many men of pride and honour would prefer revenge to any number of ounces of silver. At the time of the blood feud which led to the tragedy of Njal's Burning, Iceland had recently been converted to Christianity; but the doctrine of ready forgiveness of enemies does not appear to have sunk in very deeply; and though there are occasional references to people being 'Christian men' this never seems to have been put forward as an argument when the party who had the blood feud was being urged to accept atonement. Moreover, though in theory the acceptance of atonement ended the matter, in practice it often left some member or members of the dead man's family with a desire for more dramatic revenge, and it was easy to pick a new quarrel, leading to a brand-new feud which was really the old one in another hat.

The community was a small one and there was much inter-marriage. Both the dead man and the killer would have large numbers of relatives, all of whom would be more or less in-volved in the dispute, and would certainly be expected to support the family if the matter ever came to be discussed at the ALTHING. Throughout the Sagas there are instances of men being embarrassed to find themselves bound in honour to support both sides in the same dispute; and before the ALTHING took place, the 'drumming up' of support for one side or the other was as blatant as it is in the lobbies of the United Nations.

THE SAGA

It is against this background that the story of the burning of Njal is told in the Saga. The Sagas were first handed down from one generation to the next by word of mouth, and it is certain that Burnt Njal will not have been set down in writing until many years after the events took place, so that its exact accuracy, like that of most history, is dubious. But from the vividness of its detail and characterization no one who reads the Saga can doubt that it originally came from eye-witness accounts. This 'convincingness' of the Sagas really springs from the fact that they are always completely factual and objective. We are only told what people were seen to do and heard to say. The narrator never tries to tell us what went on in anybody's mind. We are left to infer that if we please. The result is a most curious and characteristic air of restraint which is far more moving in effect than any purple passage could be. The Norsemen could be melodramatic at times, and they had a great feeling for the heroic remark—particularly for heroic last words. Sometimes the dying hero even sings a song, full of strange 'conceits' and quite untranslatable. Here there was probably a certain amount of embroidery on the part of the narrator. But, on the whole, it is the *absence* of embroidery and melodrama which gives the Sagas their strange flavour.

In some respects the Njal Saga is an immensely complicated story with a huge cast of characters and interrelationships like a jigsaw puzzle. The reader is not helped by the fact that two characters often have the same name. Thus, Njal had an illegitimate son named Hauskuld, but he also had a *foster* son whose name was Hauskuld. We hear a good deal of Grani Gunnar's son and Gunnar Lambi's son, but Grani is not the son of Gunnar Lambi's son. It will be seen that the Saga of Burnt Njal is not altogether easy reading.

Yet in other ways the story could hardly be more starkly simple. All the complications, all the seeming irrelevancies, and all the host of minor characters are in fact a part of a magnificently woven pattern. Like a fine Persian carpet the Njal Saga produces an overwhelmingly splendid general effect from a mass of delicately executed minor motifs. And, as with the carpet, one can go on studying it for years and always finding something new.

These are things which cannot be conveyed in retelling the story briefly. The Saga tells it, with the greatest economy of language, in some three hundred and fifty pages, and there are very few pages which can be left out without sacrificing some part of the tragic inevitability of the climax and its aftermath. It is with the human and social aspects of the story that I am concerned, and on these the narrator of the Saga never comments. He records facts but never draws inferences from them.

THE CHARACTERS

We are told little or nothing of the mass of minor characters who appear in this story, except perhaps that they were the son of or cousin of somebody with a complicated name, of whom we have not heard before and never hear again. But we know a certain amount about the principal figures in the tragedy and there are some vivid little physical details about some of them.

Njal himself was nicknamed 'The Beardless Jarl', since no hair grew on his face—a thing often sneered at by his enemies. Nevertheless, he was a handsome man, though when the story begins already an old one. How old we do not know, but his age is frequently insisted on, and the story covers a period of years. He was certainly long past his physical prime. Njal was a rich landowner, and he had at least two large houses, one of which, Bergthorsknoll in the south-west of Iceland, was the scene of the climax of the story. It must have been a large house, for we know that the household consisted of over fifty people. This is not surprising, for the Norsemen frequently built themselves very big houses, and in one instance we hear of a house with a main hall two hundred feet long. The house will have been constructed entirely of wood, and probably handsomely decorated with carving.

As he appears in the story Njal is the true pattern of the elder statesman—wise, a great lawyer, liberal-minded, and with a gift, rare among the Norsemen, for foreseeing events. His contemporaries even thought he had second sight. He was much in demand for advice, which he gave freely. He was a particularly moderate and gentle man, who hated violence, but he had plenty of courage. He was extremely generous, and it was ironical that this generosity, particularly to his enemies, was one of the things that brought about his death. Njal became a Christian during the period covered by the Saga, and he seems to be almost alone amongst our characters in understanding what Christianity was really about.

His wife's name was Bergthora—a brave woman and an excellent wife and mother, but proud and quarrelsome. Throughout the story the quarrels between families often originated with the women, and frequently they egged on the men to violence. A housewife like Bergthora enjoyed high status, and could have much influence on the doings of the family.

Njal and Bergthora had three sons and three daughters. In addition, Njal had an illegitimate son named Hauskuld, who was the son of a woman named Rodny. She must have been Njal's mistress at some time, or what the Norsemen would rather charmingly have called Bergthora's 'hearth rival'. Hauskuld did not live with Njal and his family, but with his mother, and he remains throughout a rather shadowy figure. The three daughters are not of much importance to the story, and of the sons by far the most important is Skarphedinn, the eldest, a big powerful athletic man and a great fighter, but by the accounts we have of him uncommonly ugly, with a face that was ashen pale, and a very strange mouth with projecting front teeth. It is recorded that 'for the most part he kept himself well in hand', a phrase often used in the Sagas, and meaning, presumably, that he had considerable self-control. But everything we see of Skarphedinn suggests that he was quick-tongued and quick-tempered, and that like another famous person he had 'an unholy fondness for a row'. If Njal is the pattern of the wise and moderate elder statesman, then Skarphedinn is a pattern of the fighting young Norse hero of his day. His younger brothers were Grim and Helgi, and though we know that they were brave and hardy men and great fighters, they usually appear as 'supporting parts' to Skarphedinn.

Apart from Njal's own sons he had a son-in-law named Kari, a dashing, handsome, and attractive figure. Kari was the only survivor of the final massacre of Njal and his family, and the last part of the Saga is devoted to his doings as their avenger. Njal's family seems to have been a very united one, and even after his sons were married they and their wives and families continued to live with Njal, which was unusual.

We have less detailed knowledge and description of Njal's enemies, but one at least, Thrain Sigfus's son, is important, mainly because it was his death which went far to bring on the final tragedy. He was one of seven brothers, all formidable fighting men and kinsmen of the great champion Gunnar of Lithend. Thrain seems to have been a rather arrogant person, conceited and much given to outward show, but brave and often kindly. He had a son named Hauskuld, and after his death at the hands of Njal's sons, Njal, with characteristic generosity, took the young Hauskuld into his home as a foster son, thereby further complicating the relations of the blood feud, and hopelessly confusing the reader between his illegitimate son Hauskuld and his foster son Hauskuld.

But among the enemies of Njal and his family by far the most important is Flosi. He comes into the story comparatively late, when he takes up the blood feud on behalf of his niece, but from then on he is the driving force and the commander of the band who arranged and carried out the 'irredeemable crime'. Flosi is a singularly clear and convincing figure. He was a great chief and much respected as a brave, able, and powerful man. He took up the quarrel with reluctance and because he clearly felt that he had no alternative. But throughout, except when his pride is touched by some insult, he gives the impression of being a moderate, intelligent man of fundamental decency, who realized perfectly well that what he was doing was wrong, and disliked it. It would have been easy to make Flosi the villain of the story, but the Saga-teller, though on the whole his sympathies are certainly with Njal and his family, speaks of Flosi throughout with the greatest respect.

He is a fine man thrust into a terrible crime by circumstances, and as such a genuinely tragic figure.

WHAT LED UP TO THE CRIME

The Icelanders, of course, were not only great sailors but great pirates and marauders. Periodically a man or a group would go off on an expedition to Scotland, or the Orkneys, or even to Norway itself, and there spend a few months in 'harrying', either as a private enterprise or in the service of some powerful chief. It was on one such expedition that Njal's sons, Skarphedinn, Helgi, and Grim, first met Kari, who later was to become their brother-in-law, a man famous for his dash and daring, and high in favour with Earl Sigurd of the Orkneys. Through Kari's influence Njal's sons were brought into the Earl's favour.

Later in the same expedition they decided to go to Norway, and since Kari also had business in Norway with Earl Hacon, it was agreed that he and Njal's sons should meet there.

It so happened that Thrain, the eldest of the sons of Sigfus, was also at the court of Earl Hacon at the time, and was just on the point of sailing for Iceland. In the complicated series of quarrels which had led to the death of Gunnar of Lithend, Thrain's kinsman, there had been times when the kin of Njal and the kin of Gunnar had been enemies, but there is nothing to suggest that at this time there was any quarrel between Njal's sons and Thrain. One doubts if the brothers liked Thrain. They were too proud and arrogant themselves to care for other proud and arrogant people. But the immediate cause of the quarrel which now developed was a disreputable character named Hrapp. Hrapp was an Icelander who had fled to Norway after committing a murder. Whilst in Norway he robbed and burnt a shrine, whereupon Earl Hacon put a price on his head. Very much 'on the run', Hrapp came to Njal's sons and asked them to hide him from the Earl and eventually take him back to Iceland with them. This they very reasonably refused to do. Hrapp was a fellow Icelander, but he was not only a criminal but a man 'whose luck had left him'.

The idea of a man 'whose luck had left him' is a Norse concept which we shall come across again later. Such a man was to be avoided at all costs, rather as though he had an infectious disease, since he was liable to bring bad luck to anybody who had to do with him.

Refused by Njal's sons, Hrapp appealed to Thrain, whose ship was just ready to sail, and for some reason Thrain agreed to shelter him; why, is not clear. We know that Hrapp tried to bribe Thrain, and that Thrain refused. But, nevertheless, when Earl Hacon and his men arrived in search of Hrapp, Thrain concealed him. Njal's sons, who, of course, knew Hrapp was with Thrain, were questioned by the Earl about the matter, but knowing that Thrain's life was at stake they professed to know nothing about it, and eventually Thrain succeeded in sailing away with Hrapp on board.

Earl Hacon, who had been very generous to Thrain, was justifiably angry at this piece of double-dealing, and, since Thrain had now escaped, his anger turned against Njal's sons. He guessed—rightly—that Njal's sons had known that Hrapp was with Thrain, but he also seemed to have been sure that the whole thing was a plot between them and Thrain. The Earl attacked the brothers, and after a brisk fight overwhelmed them by weight of numbers, threw them into prison, and intended to kill them. They managed to break off their fetters and escape, and at this point Kari's ship arrived and they were able to take refuge with him. Kari refused to give them up to the Earl, and even seems to have persuaded him that they were innocent, for the Earl offered them atonement for the hardships they had undergone. They then started back to Iceland with Kari.

This whole incident is an excellent illustration of the Norse theory of a man 'whose luck has left him'. Hrapp, the murderer, robber, and shrine-destroyer, has now succeeded in causing trouble for everybody. It is difficult not to sympathize with Thrain in sheltering a hunted man who was a fellow countryman; yet in order to do so he has had to deceive his benefactor, the Earl. Njal's sons have acted honourably in not betraying Thrain, but it has involved them in great hardship, and nearly cost them their lives. The Earl has acted impetuously and unfairly in attacking Njal's sons, but his mistake—if it was a mistake—was a fairly natural one.

But Hrapp's 'unlucky' influence had only just begun to be felt. For when Njal's sons returned to Iceland with Kari they were in a very angry mood with Thrain, whom they considered the cause of all their troubles. It was a natural feeling, though not perhaps an entirely fair one. Thrain may have guessed that the Earl would turn on the brothers when he escaped, but he could hardly be expected to give up the chance of saving his own neck. But Njal's sons certainly thought that Thrain owed them some atonement; whilst on the other side, and now Thrain's close attendant, was Hrapp, who naturally hated the brothers for having refused to help him.

Here were the makings of a first-class quarrel, and the advice that Njal gave to his sons gives an interesting glimpse of his character. As ever, he was all for peace, and thought that it would have been better if the whole Norway business had never been mentioned when his sons returned home. But since they had become a matter of common talk he accepts that something must be done, if only as a matter of honour. He urges his sons not to call on Thrain themselves, which would almost certainly lead to a fight, but to use intermediaries to suggest that Thrain should make atonement. But there is a curiously resigned air about the advice he gives, and it is clear that he had no very great hope of a peaceful settlement and foresaw in outline, if not in detail, the coming blood feud.

However, his advice was taken. First one of Thrain's brothers and then Kari were sent as intermediaries to Thrain. Both, when they returned, refused to repeat what Thrain said. The inference is that it was something which, had the brothers heard it, would have made the quarrel even more bitter.

Eventually the brothers could no longer be restrained from going to see Thrain themselves. They were accompanied by Kari. Their reception was insultingly cold, and Thrain at once brushed aside their claim. But most of the talking was done by Hallgerda, Thrain's wife, a woman of very bad reputation, well known as a provoker of quarrels; and by Hrapp. Hallgerda insulted the brothers like a drunken fishwife, and threw in a few of the usual sneers about their father's beardlessness; while Hrapp blustered, challenged, and threatened. Only Thrain himself tried to restrain his followers and to stop the flow of insults. Skarphedinn, always quick-tongued, gave back insult for insult and threat for threat, but by the time the brothers left it was obvious that there was little chance of a peaceful settlement.

When they reached home it became even less possible; for whilst Njal still talked, without hope, of avoiding a killing, their mother, Bergthora, taunted them with what public opinion would now say. 'No one will now think that ye have the heart to lift your weapons.' Kari tried to silence her, as Thrain had tried to silence Hallgerda, but by now it was clear that the man whose luck had left him and the tongues of two quarrelsome women had done their work.

No blood had yet been shed in the quarrel, and therefore no blood feud created, but from the time of the visit of the brothers and Kari to his house Thrain knew, of course, that his life was in danger. He behaved, as he does throughout the story, as a vain, slightly stupid, but fearless man. He refused to consider the suggestion of several of his brothers that he should try to make a peaceful settlement with Njal's sons. He may have realized that any such suggestion would now certainly be refused after Hallgerda's insults. But apart from that he genuinely felt himself to be a match for them.

Nevertheless, he took certain commonsense precautions. It was no part of the Norse Code that a man need be killed in fair fight. What Thrain had mainly to fear was an ambush, and when he went on a visit he took care to have eight men with him, including Hrapp, all fully armed. Their journey meant crossing the river Markfleet, which was partly frozen over. On the banks of the river the party found some women who could not cross the river, and helped them over. Their reward for this act of kindness (for Thrain seems to have been a kind-hearted man) was that the women at once went to Njal's house at Bergthorsknoll and told Bergthora where Thrain had gone and when he would be returning. Bergthora, of course, at once passed on the information to Kari and the brothers.

After a visit of three or four days Thrain decided to return home. It was urged upon him that this would be dangerous, and even more dangerous to come back by the way he had said he would before he left home. Thrain's reply was, 'That is fear, and I will none of it.'

Early on the morning when Thrain was due to make his return journey Njal rose to find his sons armed and about to go out—Skarphedinn in a blue cape, with his famous axe called the 'Ogress of War'; Helgi in red with a red shield; and the elegant Kari in a silken jerkin with a gilded hermet, Characteristically, they had all put on bright holiday clothes. Njal asked them where they were going and they replied, laughing, that they were going on a sheep-hunt.

There were only five in the party and eight in Thrain's, and it seems that originally Njal's sons intended an attack on Thrain from ambush, just after he and his party crossed the river. But the sun glinting on their shields betrayed them, and Thrain, not knowing with how many men he had to deal, went further down the opposite bank of the river, so that to get at him the brothers had to come out into the open. Thrain and his party paused upon a tongue of ice near the bank of the river and were surprised to see only five men running down, apparently to attack them. As they did so, Skarphedinn's shoe-string broke and he stopped to retie it. The others ran on. Meanwhile Thrain, realizing that this was a serious attack, had thrown off his cloak and taken off his helmet to adjust it.

At this moment Skarphedinn, running at full speed, overtook his companions and, with a huge leap over the stream between the ice banks, shot forward, sliding on the ice, which was extremely slippery. He slid up to Thrain just as Thrain was about to put his helmet on his head, and with a single blow of the 'Ogress of War' cut his skull open right down to the teeth, 'so that his jaw teeth fell out on the ice'. The thing was done so quickly that no one could even aim a blow at him, and he slid away out of reach, leaping over a shield which one of the party threw before him on the ice. He then rejoined his brothers and Kari and they killed Hrapp and another man, but granted peace to the rest of the party, who included two—Grani Gunnar's son and Gunnar Lambi's son—who were little more than boys. It was Skarphedinn who decided that they should be spared, and one can understand his reasons, for Grani was the son of the famous Gunnar of Lithend, who had been the friend of Njal and his sons. This act of generosity, as acts of generosity in this story often were, was to be ill-repaid.

Later the brothers and Kari returned to the place where Skarphedinn had made his leap and found that it measured twenty-four feet. On this Sir George Dasent comments 'a good jump, but not beyond the power of man'. A jump of twenty-four feet is not, of course, beyond the power of a first-class long-jumper from a prepared track and take-off. One would certainly have thought it was beyond the power of an armed man carrying an axe and jumping off a river bank. Again, a first-class ice-hockey player might slide past an opponent and cut his skull in half with a single blow. There are ice-hockey matches in which something of the kind seems to be the main object of the game. Perhaps it is a mistake to be too solemn about accounts of heroic feats of arms. We are told that Skarphedinn was a quite exceptionally powerful and nimble man, and on this showing he certainly was.

However, with Thrain and Hrapp both dead, Njal's sons were avenged; and since some of Thrain's brothers, the other sons of Sigfus, had never felt that he was entirely in the right

in the quarrel, it was now possible for Njal to offer atonement
of money for Thrain's death, and for it to be accepted. The
usual pledges of peace and good faith were agreed to by both
parties, and for the time being, at least, the quarrel seemed to
be at an end.

It was at this point that Njal made one of his characteristically generous gestures. Thrain had a son named Hauskuld
(not to be confused with Njal's son Hauskuld). He was a
handsome, intelligent, and attractive boy. Njal visited him and
asked him if he knew how his father died. The boy replied
that he knew that Skarphedinn had killed him, but that since
atonement had been accepted it was not a matter which should
be talked about. This reply, according to Norse etiquette, was in
excellent taste, and Njal's comment was 'better answered than
asked'. Njal decided that Hauskuld had the makings of a fine
man and adopted him as his foster son. Over the next few years
Hauskuld grew up in the company of Njal's sons, and everything that we hear of him suggests that Njal's prophecy had
been right. Hauskuld certainly became a most admirable man,
and much beloved—particularly, we are told, by Njal's sons,
from whom he was inseparable.

*   *   *   *

This happy and peaceful state of affairs must have gone on
for some years—years during which Hauskuld was growing
from a boy to a man—and during this time there was no re-
currence of the old quarrel. Njal spoke with quiet pride at the
THING about the completeness of the reconciliation, giving it as
an example of what could be achieved by moderation and
goodwill; and when Njal rode eastward on important business
he was accompanied not only by his own sons and Kari but by
the sons of Sigfus, the dead Thrain's brothers.

The important business that took Njal to the east was the
quest for a wife for Hauskuld, his foster son. Njal wished to
marry Hauskuld to Hildigunna, who was the niece of Flosi,
a great and powerful chief. Flosi welcomed Njal heartily, and

in principle seemed in favour of the match; but Hildigunna herself, a spirited young woman, insisted that if she was to marry Hauskuld he must have some standing in the community, such as a 'priesthood'. Njal said he would try to arrange this, and further talk about the marriage was postponed while he did so.

A 'priest' in Iceland at that time was a sort of area leader, who was responsible for various duties in the organization of the THINGS, and in the days of the old religion he had been in charge of the temple rites. Iceland had only become Christian within the last few years, and it is not quite clear whether the priest any longer had spiritual duties. But he was certainly a man of importance, and there were only about fifty priests in the whole country. What Hildigunna was asking for would be roughly the equivalent of a woman today demanding that her prospective husband should have a title.

It was permissible to sell a priesthood, but Njal could not find a seller. He solved the problem characteristically. The courts of the THINGS had been overcrowded with suits, so that it was impossible to get a ruling on a dispute without long delay. Njal suggested to the ALTHING that to speed matters up a new court should be created, which in turn would mean the creation of new priesthoods. When this was agreed Njal asked for a new priesthood to be set up at Whiteness for his foster son Hauskuld. Though Hauskuld was now a grown man, he must have been unusually young to be a priest, and it says much for the influence of Njal and the general respect for Hauskuld himself that he was appointed. Thereafter he was known as Hauskuld the Priest of Whiteness (to the relief of any reader of the Saga, who at last has some means of distinguishing between him and Hauskuld, Njal's son).

There was now no barrier to the marriage with Hildigunna, and it duly took place at Flosi's home. Hauskuld and Hildigunna then returned to Bergthorsknoll with Njal, and we hear (perhaps with just a faint note of surprise) that all went well between Hildigunna and Bergthora. But in the next spring

Njal bought an estate for Hauskuld and he and Hildigunna
set up their own home.

The period that followed is perhaps the happiest in the whole
story. The wisdom and moderation of Njal seemed to have
triumphed everywhere. The blood feud with the sons of Sigfus
had been composed (one of them, indeed, was now Njal's
son-in-law). Njal's generosity in taking the dead Thrain's son
into his household had been well regarded, for not only had
Hauskuld made an excellent match and obtained an important
public position, but we are repeatedly told of the warmth of
the friendship between the households of Njal and of Hauskuld
the Priest of Whiteness.

Exactly how long this sunny period went on we do not know,
but we are told it was 'for a long while'. Then not only is the
sun darkened but a curious mist comes over the scene. Until
now everybody's motives have been reasonably clear—even
those of the disastrous Hrapp. Later in the story motives are
to become clear again. But for the moment what happens is
puzzling.

A man named Lyting was married to the sister of the dead
Thrain. She will therefore have been the aunt of Hauskuld the
Priest of Whiteness. Lyting's farm was not far from that of
Njal's illegitimate son Hauskuld and his mother, and to get
to his own farm from Bergthorsknoll, Njal's son had to ride
past Lyting's farm. It is not suggested that he trespassed on
Lyting's property. He just often rode past it. This seems to
have annoyed Lyting so much that he gave a feast at his house,
to which he invited Hauskuld the Priest of Whiteness and the
sons of Sigfus, and suggested that they should kill Hauskuld,
Njal's son, in revenge for the death of Thrain. They all indignantly refused to break the atonement that had been made;
Hauskuld, Priest of Whiteness, in particular, saying that it
would be returning Njal, his foster father, much evil for much
good. They left the feast in anger. Lyting, however, claimed
that he had never accepted atonement for Thrain, and shortly
after he, with his two brothers and three of his housecarls,

laid an ambush for Hauskuld, Njal's son, and as he rode by the six of them set upon him and, after a severe fight, killed him. They do not appear to have proclaimed the slaying in the proper way, but made off and hid themselves in the woods.

This was not only a peculiarly dastardly and cowardly murder but one so stupid and pointless that one wonders whether the account of it which the Saga gives us is the whole truth. Even in tenth-century Iceland it was unusual to kill a man merely for riding by your farm; and Lyting's claim that he had taken no atonement for Thrain, even if it were true, would be a very poor excuse for reopening the blood feud when neither Thrain's brothers nor his son were prepared to do so. Moreover, no man in his senses would have wanted to reopen, quite unnecessarily, a blood feud with Njal's sons and Kari, about the most formidable men in the country.

The body of Hauskuld was brought to his mother, Rodny, who took it on a sledge to Bergthorsknoll. She did not close the eyes or nostrils of the body, leaving that to Skarphedinn, and placing in his hands also the duty of avenging his half-brother. We should not have expected Bergthora to be very keen to risk the lives of her own sons to avenge the son of her 'hearth rival', but as usual she was all for revenge. Her one worry was that Hauskuld the Priest of Whiteness, when he heard of the murder, would offer atonement, and that it might be accepted.

Skarphedinn and his brothers agreed with her, and this is a further puzzling point in the whole business; for from the moment that revenge was decided upon, it seems to have been taken for granted that the victim must be Hauskuld the Priest. This seems quite irrational. Hauskuld the Priest had taken no part in the murder, and had, in fact, indignantly refused to do so. He and Njal's sons had been brought up together, and we are repeatedly told of the unusual warmth and completeness of their friendship. He was only related by marriage to the actual murderer. Why, then, was he selected as the target?

There seem to be two possible explanations. The first is that

Skarphedinn and his brothers believed, rightly or wrongly, that Hauskuld the Priest had been privy to the murder of their half-brother—in other words, that Lyting was no more than a tool in the affair. The only possible evidence of this is that Hauskuld the Priest did not warn Njal's family of Lyting's proposal to him but contented himself with refusing to have anything to do with it and riding away. But it seems most unlikely, from all we hear of Hauskuld the Priest, that he had any hand in the murder, direct or indirect. He appears to have been a man of outstanding character, and an intelligent one— the last person to be mixed up in a brutal and completely pointless murder. On the other hand, it is possible, though there is no evidence for it, that some of the other sons of Sigfus or their relatives may have been secretly involved, since we know from what happened later that some of them were irresponsible and treacherous.

A much more probable reason for the selection of Hauskuld the Priest as an object of vengeance would be that the friendship between him and Njal's sons was not as complete as we are told it was. The brothers may have been jealous of Hauskuld. Njal had treated him like a particularly beloved youngest son, been very generous to him, and gained him an important position. Hauskuld appears in many ways to have been much more like Njal in nature and outlook than were Skarphedinn and his brothers, and after Hauskuld's death Njal said publicly at the THING that he would rather have lost all his own sons than that Hauskuld should have been killed. If that was really his attitude, jealousy on the part of his own sons would have been very natural. So would jealousy on the part of Bergthora when she saw Njal's affection for one who was not her son and who was brought into the household without consultation with her.

But whether Njal's family was jealous of Hauskuld or not there were other people who certainly were, and these were constantly slandering Hauskuld to Njal's sons.

There now seems to have been a pause. We are told that

the spring was early and the men were busy sowing their corn. This is the probable explanation for most of the strange pauses in the story. Murder, as war has often had to do, must wait until the farming seasons allowed time for it. Perhaps also the brothers secretly realized that to kill Hauskuld would be well below even their cheerfully murderous standards.

But in the end the pressure of the slanderers was too strong, and early one morning Njal's sons, Kari, and a man named Mord, who hated Hauskuld, rode to Ossaby, the home of the Priest of Whiteness. There they ambushed him, in much the same way as Hauskuld Njal's son had been ambushed—five men attacking him without warning and cutting him down. As he fell he said, 'God help me, and forgive you!' All the five gave him wounds, as they had sworn to do. This was not mere barbarity, but to make sure that all accepted an equal degree of responsibility for the killing. Hauskuld's blood saturated the cloak that he was wearing, a gift from Flosi.

It is a far cry from the great feat of arms when Thrain was killed on the ice of the Markfleet, and five men had attacked and defeated eight in open fight, to this cold-blooded murder of one innocent man by five. For the first time Njal's sons cease to be fighting heroes and became mere thugs. They had killed Thrain, and now they had killed his son and their own foster brother. When Njal heard the news he wept, not only for his beloved Hauskuld but for 'what would come after'. 'What will come after?' says Skarphedinn. 'My death,' says Njal, 'and the death of my wife and all my sons.' Men believed that Njal had second sight. He may have had, but he would scarcely have needed it to make this prophecy.

*   *   *   *

One of the many particularly ugly aspects of the murder of Hauskuld the Priest was that the brothers and Mord had agreed that though Mord himself had been one of the murderers, he should be kept out of the matter altogether, and in the meantime, being a well-known expert in law, put himself forward to prepare the case for Hauskuld's next of kin. It was as though one member of a gang of criminals were to seek the job of solicitor to the prosecution; and the effect would be that when it was revealed that Mord was one of the murderers the whole pleading of the suit would be completely irregular and the prosecution would be bound to fail. This cunning trick worked admirably, and Mord was duly appointed by Hauskuld's family to put forward the suit on their behalf.

The news of the murder of Hauskuld had by now reached Flosi, and he came to visit the widowed Hildigunna, his niece. The Norsemen respected their wives, and treated them exceptionally well, but they do not seem to have been great romantic lovers, and there is very little in the Sagas about passionate love between men and women, although there is plenty about married loyalty. Perhaps this is in line with the usual tendency of the Sagas to say nothing about people's inner feelings. There seems no doubt that Hildigunna had genuinely loved Hauskuld, and, as we have already seen, she was a high-spirited woman. But she was that type of Norse-woman, like Bergthora and Rodny and Hallgerda, who believed that the only proper answer to one murder was another, or preferably several. She set the scene for her meeting with Flosi with some care, and, entering weeping, asked him point-blank what vengeance or help she should have of him. Flosi promised her that he would help her to the limit of the law, but it was clear that the law was not what Hildigunna wanted. Going to her chest, she took out the cloak, Flosi's gift, that Hauskuld had been wearing when he was killed, and which she had kept locked up complete with the blood that soaked it. Then, going silently up behind Flosi, she threw the cloak over him so that the dried blood rattled down all over him, and called on him to take vengeance for Hauskuld or else to be called a dastard. Flosi was naturally angry and shaken. 'He flushed hotly and then turned ashen pale.' Hurling the cloak back at her he called her a hell hag, and recalled the Norse saying that 'woman's counsel is ever cruel'. With that he left her, and went away to consult with the other parties who would now inherit the blood feud—the sons of Sigfus, Thrain's brothers and uncles of the murdered Hauskuld.

Their attitude seems to have been much the same as Flosi's own—they would pursue the suit to the utmost, but peacefully and legally. One of them, Kettle of the Mark, was in a particularly difficult position, since whilst he was Hauskuld's uncle, he was also Njal's son-in-law. The only two of the group who were for violent revenge were Grani Gunnar's son and Lambi Sigurd's son, the two younger men who, as youngsters, had been spared by Skarphedinn's generosity in the fight in which Thrain was killed. They appear throughout the story as a thoroughly unpleasant pair, and Flosi obviously had little use for them. He told them sharply, as he was to tell them again later, that their talk was greater than their courage, and that what they were asking for was something that they would bitterly regret later. Flosi was intelligent enough to see that to continue the blood feud could only end in disaster for all concerned.

The suit therefore came to be tried at the THING, and beforehand, in the usual way, both sides were busy rallying their supporters and canvassing for others. It was obvious that Njal's sons were likely to be in trouble, since Flosi, his followers and relatives, and the sons of Sigfus formed an extremely powerful group, and public opinion, for what it was worth, had been greatly shocked by the murder of Hauskuld. The scene in the Saga in which the brothers and their friend Asgrim go from booth to booth asking for help and support in the suit has a most extraordinary quality of impending tragedy. At each booth the same thing happens, with little variation. Asgrim appeals for help on behalf of the brothers, and help is refused with varying degrees of politeness and rudeness. But in each instance the man appealed to looks at Skarphedinn and asks about him in a curious form of words. 'Who is that man,' they say, 'with the axe on his shoulder, before whom four men walk? A big well-made, pale-faced, ugly man? He looks a good fighting man, but I think his luck has left him.' Obviously these people really knew Skarphedinn well by sight, but these words were a sort of formal expression of the idea that, since Skarphedinn's 'luck had left him', he was to be avoided, as the brothers themselves had felt about Hrapp. It was not exactly an insult, but it was certainly not a pleasant thing to be told. Skarphedinn's replies, as ever, were sharp and contemptuous, and on some occasions the discussion nearly ended in a fight. When the brothers returned to Njal with little hope of support he took the news resignedly, with the quiet comment, 'Things draw on now to what must be.'

There were still many influential men who were working for agreement and the payment of an atonement without the suit coming before the courts. But Flosi and his followers, though wishing to avoid more killings, were determined to get what satisfaction they could in law. If the suit could be properly pleaded and proved (and the brothers' responsibility for the killing of Hauskuld was not in dispute) this might mean that Njal's sons would be proclaimed outlaws, when they could be killed at any time out of hand without incurring any penalty.

The suit was opened before the THING, and what we may call the witnesses for the prosecution gave their evidence. But when this evidence was finished Mord's trap was sprung. A speaker on behalf of the brothers revealed that Mord had been one of the murderers and that he had also been the man to give notice of the suit, which was, of course, completely irregular and illegal, and meant that the suit must fall to the ground. This was a triumph for Mord's cunning, but it meant a highly explosive situation. If Flosi and his party found themselves denied all justice by a piece of barefaced cheating, the blood feud would certainly go on.

At this point, however, Njal intervened. Although it appeared that the suit was bad in law, he said, he wished to offer atonement for Hauskuld's death on behalf of his sons. He would rather have lost all his own sons than that Hauskuld should have been killed.

Flosi was now in a difficult position. Previously he had steadily refused to accept private atonement, preferring that the THING should make its decision. But now he was left with the alternative of accepting atonement or leaving Hauskuld unatoned and continuing the blood feud. Strong pressure was put on him to accept Njal's offer, and in the end he did so—or, at least, seemed to do so. The main reason he gave for his decision was his personal respect for Njal, which is puzzling in view of what happened later.

Each side now appointed its 'daymen' or umpires, six from each side forming the committee which would determine the award, and there was then a good deal of handshaking and rather sudden mutual regard.

The committee of daysmen conferred and decided that Hauskuld should be atoned by a payment of six hundred ounces of silver. This was a very large sum—at least three times as much as would usually have been paid for a man of high standing. It was fixed so high both as a tribute to Hauskuld and to mark the general disapproval of his killing. Moreover, the money was to be paid down at once at the THING.

This was a difficulty, since even a rich man like Njal would hardly travel with six hundred ounces of silver. But the difficulty was overcome in an interesting and highly significant way. Njal and his sons put down what money they had with them, which amounted to two hundred ounces of silver. The remaining four hundred ounces was provided by subscription from the twelve daysmen themselves. There is no previous record of this having been done, and, apart from its generosity, shows a sense of public interest in settling the dispute. Even a thousand years ago the Norsemen seem to have been groping towards the idea that society is indivisible and that peace is a matter of public interest.

Njal was well satisfied with the award, but we are told that Skarphedinn made no comment but a scornful smile. This we can understand. The award and the method of paying it were an ingenious effort to keep the peace, but two proud and angry men like Skarphedinn and Flosi will hardly have liked it. Skarphedinn may have resented the idea of the atonement for his deed being raised by something like public charity, while Flosi will certainly have noticed that whereas three times the usual sum was being paid in atonement for Hauskuld, only one-third of this was being paid by Njal and his sons.

Such feelings may explain what now happened. The money, as usual in such cases, was weighed out publicly—probably in the form of spiral bands of silver rather resembling bracelets. It would now be Flosi's part to take the money for division amongst those to whom it was due, and at the same time there would be more back-slapping and declarations of peace and future friendliness. Here, however, Njal made a charming, characteristic, and fatal mistake. He took a silken scarf and a pair of boots and added them to the heap of money. These things were intended, of course, as a gesture of goodwill—a personal present as opposed to the mere formal payment of the award. Flosi, however, at once picked on the scarf and scornfully demanded who had given it. Skarphedinn ask him curtly whom he thought. Flosi replied with a sneer that he supposed it must have been Njal, for it was a womanly thing, and to look at Njal with no hair on his face many men did not know whether he was a man or a woman.

This cheap, worn-out insult at such a time, coming soon after Flosi had publicly said that this reason for accepting the atonement was his respect for Njal, can only be explained if he wished to wreck the negotiations. Skarphedinn replied angrily and rather splendidly that it was unworthy to sneer at an old man, and that Flosi might be quite sure that Njal was a man, for he had had sons who had never failed to take vengeance for the deaths of *their* kinsmen. He then took the silken scarf himself and threw a pair of breeches to Flosi, saying that he needed them, and when Flosi asked why, jeeringly replied, 'Because thou art the mistress of the Swinefells goblin, if, as men say, he does indeed turn thee into a woman every ninth night.' Breeches, or any similar closed garment, had a strong sexual significance for the Norsemen. A woman could be divorced for wearing them, just as a man could be divorced for wearing a shirt which was too open at the front and therefore 'womanly'. Skarphedinn's gesture and words amounted to suggesting that Flosi was a homosexual and a warlock, and they brought the whole reconciliation to an end with a bang. Flosi refused to touch the money, saying that Hauskuld should either fall unatoned or that he would have vengeance for him. He would now neither give nor take peace, and he and his party rode away from the THING. So did Njal and his sons, Njal, at least, with a heavy heart. Probably he was not really surprised, but the doom he had foreseen when Hauskuld was killed now seemed certain. Skarphedinn pointed out cheerfully that Flosi's party could no longer pursue them by the law of the land. Perhaps to the man of action, who neither knew nor cared about the law, but was quite confident that his hands could keep his head, this was a happy reflection. But Njal's comment was 'Then that will happen which will be worse for all of us.'

In the meantime the daysmen at the THING who had worked so hard for peace were left in the awkward position of having six hundred ounces of silver with nobody to claim it. It was suggested that those who had contributed should take their money back, but in Norse etiquette to take back anything which one had freely given was dishonourable. As one of the subscribers put it, 'That shame I will never choose for myself, to take back what I have given away, either here or elsewhere.' It was eventually decided that the money should be divided into two halves and put in the keeping of two of the daysmen, one from each party, until the next ALTHING, on the general principle of the raincheck. There was an uneasy feeling on the part of all that it would not be long before that money would be needed to atone for *something*.

So the pacific house of cards painstakingly built by Njal and the wiser men on both sides had finally collapsed. The immediate cause of the collapse was the pride and quick temper of

Skarphedinn on one side and Flosi on the other, and it is wryly
amusing that amongst the virtues attributed to both of them
was the ability 'to keep himself well in hand'. But perhaps
more important than these individual failings was the failure
of the THING as an instrument of social justice. Flosi had
steadily refused to pursue the blood feud, and had insisted on
proceeding by law. His reward for this had been to be called a
coward by Hildigunna. Yet when the suit comes to the THING
Flosi finds that his glaringly obvious case can be set aside
purely by a piece of 'legal' chicanery. What Flosi was asking
for was justice and the proper punishment of the offenders.
He was refused justice, and though he was offered a large sum
of money instead, two-thirds of this money was not to come
from the guilty parties but by public subscription. He must
have felt that in the most literal sense Njal's sons were 'getting
away with murder'. Flosi was a serious-minded man, and he
may have felt, however vaguely, that there was something more
than his personal honour at stake—as indeed there was.
Society, as represented by the THING, had shown goodwill,
generosity, the desire for peace, and even a sense of public
responsibility. What it had not shown, and what its imperfect
laws and lack of organization had made it impossible for it to
show, was either justice or authority.

THE PLANNING AND EXECUTION
OF THE GREAT CRIME

Immediately after the final quarrel at the THING Flosi called a
meeting of his followers and the sons of Sigfus, and asked them
what they now had in mind. That dubious young pair, Grani
Gunnar's son and Gunnar Lambi's son, of course, clamoured
that nothing would please them until Njal's sons were dead.
This time, however, opinion seems to have been unanimously
on their side. Even Kettle of the Mark, Njal's son-in-law, who
had always been steadfastly on the side of peace, now agreed
that there was no alternative. There is no doubt that Flosi's

party now felt that not only their family honour but their lives were at stake, being in a blood feud with men as formidable as Njal's sons.

There were no less than one hundred and twenty men at the meeting and Flosi first demanded that they should elect a leader. It was a more or less formal question, since Flosi himself, by birth, power, and ability, was the obvious choice, and he was unanimously elected. He made them all swear an oath to him that only death should end their partnership, and that anybody who quitted the quarrel before it was over should forfeit his life and his land. It should be noted that amongst those who took this oath was Ingialld, who was the brother of Rodny, the mother of Njal's illegitimate son Hauskuld.

Having had his leadership confirmed and bound his followers to him by oath, Flosi set out his plans. Every man should return home and go on with his work during the summer until the end of haymaking time (once again that characteristic pause to get on with the farm work). Then on a stated day Flosi would ride from his home in the east to a certain rendezvous, riding very fast by means of each man having two horses, and there the whole party of one hundred and twenty would meet. Before Flosi left home a Mass was to be sung for him, and this is a sudden and startling reminder that these men had recently become Christians. The gathering was to take place at about six o'clock in the evening and thereafter the party would ride to Bergthorsknoll and 'fall on Njal's sons with fire and sword, and not turn away before they were all dead'. If anyone who had joined in the quarrel and taken the oath did not come, then, Flosi adds grimly, 'that man shall lose nothing save his life'. The plan was, of course, to be kept secret at all costs, 'for our lives lie on it'.

Up to a point the plan was intelligent and well conceived— at least as far as the rendezvous was concerned. But there is no clear plan of how the attack is to be made when they reach Njal's house; and to leave a vital secret in the hands of a hundred and twenty men over a period of weeks meant a big risk that the plan would be betrayed, which would give their enemies a chance to attack and destroy them in detail.

In fact the existence of the plan, if not its details, *was* betrayed through one of those intermarriage mix-ups that we have encountered several times before. There had apparently been rumours of an intending attack on Njal's sons, and Rodny questioned her brother Ingialld, one of those who had taken the oath to Flosi, about it. Ingialld admitted that there was a conspiracy and an oath, and Rodny reproached him for taking part in a conspiracy against Njal, who had been very good to him. Ingialld eventually promised her that though under the oath that they had sworn it might cost him his life, he would not take part in any action against Njal and his family. But he utterly refused, as a man of honour, to tell her any details of the plan.

This only appears to have happened in the late summer, so that there was little time for Njal and his sons to take any unusual action, even if they had wished to do so. They would, of course, have realized from the time of the parting at the THING that their lives were in danger. Njal had suggested to Kari that he should go to his own home, but Kari had refused, insisting that he would stand by the brothers whatever happened. There were thirty fighting men in Njal's household, and they may reasonably have felt that they could deal with any likely attack.

At this time, as ever before great events, there were various portents and prophesyings. One man went out at night and heard an enormous crash which seemed to shake the earth. Then he saw in the air a fiery ring, and within it a man on a grey horse, riding hard. The man was black and carried a flaming firebrand. The man sang a riddling song in which Flosi's name frequently occurred. Then he hurled the firebrand towards the fells and there was an enormous blaze of fire into which the man rode and vanished.

More practical and to the point was an old woman who

worked at Bergthorsknoll and who was slightly mad. One day she was found beating a vetch-stack with a cudgel and calling it a wretch. When asked why, she said that the stack would be used to set fire to the house, when all within it would be burnt, and clamoured for it to be taken away to the water or burnt up as quickly as possible. The old lady may have been mad, but there was certainly common sense in what she suggested, and she proved to be a better tactician than Skarphedinn, who only laughed at her and said that if a fire were foredoomed something else would be got to light it, even if the stack were not there.

Nowadays we find this fatalistic, unorganized, almost happy-go-lucky, attitude on the part of Skarphedinn and others rather surprising. Njal's family now knew by common sense, by rumour, and by Rodny's information that they were going to be attacked, although they did not know exactly when. But they do not seem to have done anything in particular to organize their defences; whilst on the other side we have already seen that Flosi had no clear plan about how the attack was to be carried out once he and his party reached Bergthorsknoll. This was partly the fatalistic Norse attitude that what was foredoomed would happen anyhow. But the Norsemen, with certain notable exceptions like Njal, were not given to careful forethought and planning, and certainly not in regard to battle. To them a fight was something in which the only grand principle was to hit the other man harder and more quickly than he could hit you. Anything beyond that was likely to be some glorious piece of improvisation, like Skarphedinn's slide over the ice to kill Thrain.

At the day and time appointed Flosi rode from the east with his men to the rendezvous. All who had taken the oath were there except Ingialld, who had broken his oath in order to keep his promise to Rodny not to take part in the attack. At the time when they were assembling, Skarphedinn's brothers, Grim and Helgi, were away from home. But the gathering of as large a body as a hundred and twenty men could not be kept secret, and the news of it was brought to the brothers, who at once hurried home to Bergthorsknoll.

It must have been a nerve-racking evening for the family, for everyone knew that the attack might now take place at any moment, and Bergthora said openly that each should choose his own food, since it was the last evening that she would set food before her household. Njal, too, had a vision in which he saw the gable wall of the house come down and the whole table a mass of blood. It was Skarphedinn who in this gloomy atmosphere told everybody to cheer up, and reminded them of the bearing that men would expect of them. Skarphedinn was obviously one of those men whose spirits tend to rise in danger, as on the occasion when he put on his holiday clothes before going out to kill Thrain.

Before setting out, Flosi made his men go into a church and pray. It would be interesting to know what they prayed for. Success, forgiveness, or both? They then rode to Bergthorsknoll, tethered their horses out of sight from the house, and stayed there till dusk was falling. Then on Flosi's orders they walked slowly towards the house in close order. Flosi admitted that this was to see what Njal and his family would do. He still had no clear plan of his own.

When the party was seen approaching, Njal and his sons and Kari and all the fighting men of the household, some thirty in all, came out of the house and stood in array in the yard. At this Flosi halted and considered his tactics. He was not at all anxious to attack the household forces whilst they were in the open.

This unwillingness to attack seems strange in a man of Flosi's courage, when he outnumbered his opponents by four to one, but there were good reasons for it. The 'yard' will have been a sort of stockade which gave the defenders some protection—particularly against being surrounded. Moreover, as when the brothers and Kari had beaten Thrain and seven other men, a Norse fight was usually won by the quality of the fighters rather than by their numbers. Njal's sons and

Kari were all famous and formidable men. Flosi had no group in his band who were likely to have been their individual match, and he knew quite well that some of the men with him had mouths bigger than their hearts. Both sides consisted largely of serving men, and whereas Njal's might be expected to fight hard in defence of their home ground, as King Harold's housecarls did at Hastings, Flosi's own would not feel much enthusiasm about risking their lives in their master's blood feud.

Had the defenders remained in the open, no one can say what might have happened. Flosi himself was certainly doubtful. But at this point Njal, a better stateman than a soldier, gave orders that the defenders should withdraw indoors. The reason he gave was that when Gunnar of Lithend had been attacked in his house the large band that attacked him had had desperately hard work to overcome him, though he was alone. Skarphedinn at once protested. Gunnar had been able to put up such a defence from inside his house 'because those who attacked him were too noble-minded to set fire to the house with him in it'. He was sure that Flosi and his band would have no such scruples if they could not win in any other way. 'Besides,' he added, 'I am unwilling to let myself be stifled indoors like a fox in his earth.'

The point behind this argument was not only a tactical but a moral one. There were a certain number of acts which in the Norse Code were called Nithling—that is to say, 'irredeemable crimes' which could not be atoned in the usual way; and, of these, to burn a man in his house was one. It was an act which was regarded with peculiar horror. Whilst tactically Skarphedinn was undoubtedly right, therefore, Njal, with his tendency to expect people to be more civilized than they were, may well have believed that the burning of the house was a crime which Flosi would never stoop to commit.

Njal was deeply hurt that his orders should be questioned, and complained that now he was old, his sons had ceased to honour him. At this the sons gave way. 'Let us do as our father wills,' says Helgi. 'That will be best.' 'I am not so sure of that,' says Skarphedinn, 'for now is he "fey". But still I may well humour my father in this, being burnt indoors along with him, for I am not afraid of my death.' Then as the party withdrew indoors Skarphedinn and Kari made a pact to stand or fall together and to avenge one another if only one of them should survive.

As soon as the defenders were indoors Flosi attacked and made an attempt to take the house by storm, reminding his men that at all costs none of Njal's sons or Kari must get away. Throughout the whole business Flosi was always obsessed with this fear that there might be a survivor of the attack who would then be able to carry on the blood feud. It was a very sensible fear, for once Flosi's band had been broken up and its members had gone to their homes, one determined man might easily do them tremendous harm by a series of separate attacks.

The attempt to storm the house was a total failure. At least one of Flosi's men was killed by Skarphedinn, and a number were wounded by spears thrown from the house. As the Saga puts it, 'Flosi and his men could do nothing.'

Flosi was now faced with a terrible dilemma. He could not take the house by storm, and he dared not withdraw and face the future vengeance of Njal's sons and Kari. To get rid of them once and for all had been the whole object of the conspiracy and the attack. There was now nothing for it but to set fire to the house; and this he shrank from, not only because it was Nithling, the 'irredeemable crime', but because it was 'a deed which we shall have to answer for heavily before God, since we are Christian men ourselves'. We remember that Flosi, unlike most of the recent Norse converts, seems to have taken Christianity seriously, and that he had had a Mass sung before he left home, and had taken his men to church to pray before they set out to Bergthorsknoll. Yet it is significant that when the attack was first proposed he had said that they would fall on the sons of Njal with 'fire and sword'. He was probably quite sincere in his dislike of the idea of setting fire to the house, but he must have realized from the beginning, as Skarphedinn clearly did, that it might come to that in the end; and Flosi was not the man to leave a job unfinished.

He therefore gave orders to set the house on fire, and his men began to light huge fires outside the doors. Skarphedinn characteristically called out to them to know whether they were taking to cooking. The unpleasant Grani Gunnar's son replied that they were, and that Sharphedinn would not need to be better done.

For a while the attempts to set fire to the house failed, though it was, of course, entirely constructed of wood. The defenders threw water and wey and slops on it, so that it made little progress. Then one of Flosi's men noticed the vetch-stack near the house and suggested that it could be used to start a fire in a loft over the hall, and before the defenders noticed it the whole roof of the hall was ablaze. The frightened women began to wail, but Njal comforted them, telling them to put their faith in God, 'who is so merciful that He will not let us burn both in this world and the next'.

The whole house was now blazing and it was obvious that the defence could not go on. Njal therefore went to the door and called through it to Flosi, asking him whether he would accept atonement or whether he would let anybody go out unharmed. Flosi replied with terrible finality that he would not accept atonement, that he intended to end his dealings with Njal's sons once and for all, and that he would not stir from the spot until they were all dead. But he would allow the women and children and housecarls to come out. Njal then urged them all to go, and they did, except Bergthora, and Kari's little son, who refused to leave his grandmother, whether because he was too brave or too frightened one cannot say.

As the women were going out an attempt was made to smuggle Helgi out with them, with a woman's cloak thrown over him and a handkerchief bound round his head. The idea, of course, was not merely to save Helgi's life but to get some male member of the family out so that vengeance might be taken later. But Helgi was a big broad-shouldered man and Flosi at once saw through the trick. Helgi threw off the cloak and fought hard for his life, but Flosi, coming up, cut off his head with a single blow.

Flosi now went to the door again and called to Njal, offering him leave to come out, 'for it was not fitting that he should burn indoors'. Njal quietly refused. He was too old, he said, to avenge his sons but he would not live in shame (as he would have felt that he was doing had he survived them and left them unavenged). Flosi then invited Bergthora to come out, but she too refused. 'I was given away to Njal young, and I have promised him this, that we should both share the same fate.'

Then Njal said to Bergthora: 'We will go to our bed and lay us down. I have long been eager for rest.' They then went to their bed and lay down with Kari's little boy between them, and on Njal's instructions his steward covered them completely with the hide of an ox which had recently been slaughtered. They did not speak or move again. When Skarphedinn saw his father and mother lie down he said, 'Our father goes early to bed, and that is to be looked for, for he is an old man.'

The steward had now escaped from the house, so that apart from Njal and Bergthora and the boy, there remained only Skarphedinn, Grim, and Kari, who were still fighting hard. But now the big beams from the roof began to fall, and Flosi drew back his men and left the fire to finish the work.

One of the big cross-beams had burnt through the middle and come down so that one end of it was on the floor of the hall and the other still propped high against the wall. Kari called to Skarphedinn and told him to run up the cross-beam and jump out from its top end, but Skarphedinn insisted that Kari should go first, saying that he would follow close behind him. Kari hesitated to leave him, but Skarphedinn urged him to go and, if he got away, to avenge him. Kari then took up a blazing bench and threw it into the courtyard. While the attention of Flossi and his men was distracted by the blazing bench flying out among them, Kari leaped down from the roof. His clothes were on fire and his hair singed away, but he crept away hidden by the smoke, and, running to a stream, threw himself down into it and so put out his burning clothes, and escaped into the darkness.

As soon as Kari had jumped, Skarphedinn tried in turn to run up the cross-beam, but it broke down under him. He tried to scramble up the wall, but that too gave way and he fell down again. Then Skarphedinn said, 'Now one can see what will come,' and started to try to work his way along the side wall to find his brother Grim; but as he reached him Grim fell dead —probably from asphyxiation. Then the whole of the remainder of the roof fell in, so that Skarphedinn was trapped between it and the wall.

Flosi and his band stayed by the fire until daylight. Whilst they were still there a man rode up and asked what had been happening and who had died in the fire. Flosi replied that Njal and Bergthora and all their sons and Kari and his son were certainly dead. The man replied that that could hardly be, since a few hours before he had met Kari and lent him a horse. Kari's hair and his upper clothes had been burnt off him, and one edge of his sword, 'Lifeluller', had been blue with fire and softened. But Kari had said that he would harden it in the blood of the sons of Sigfus and the other burners.

This must have been a terrible moment for Flosi, for it meant that the one thing that he had always feared had happened: a young, vigorous, and most formidable warrior had survived the attack. Flosi had staked everything on a final settlement with Njal's family by one tremendous blow. In doing so he had committed Nithling as a Norseman and a mortal sin as a Christian. With the escape of Kari he had failed.

*   *   *   *

Although the burners were a band of a hundred and twenty men, Flosi realized at once that they were now in mortal danger—particularly if they did not keep together—and he urged that the sons of Sigfus should ride east with him to his home. Some wanted to search the ruins of the house for the body of Skarphedinn and the others, but Flosi insisted that they should get away as quickly as they could before Kari could raise the whole countryside against them. Being from the east, Flosi was to some extent a 'foreigner' in south-west Iceland, so that even those who might not have had much sympathy with Njal's sons would regard the burning as a sort of invasion.

On their way the band paused to take vengeance, as they had sworn to do, on Ingialld for his broken oath. They came upon him riding on the opposite bank of a river, and Flosi threw a spear at him and wounded him. But Ingialld threw the spear back and killed one of Flosi's followers and escaped into the woods. They could not spare the time to hunt him down and rode hastily away; not, however, heading east, as they knew that was what their enemies would expect them to do.

Meanwhile Kari had raised a large band of kinsmen and sympathizers to hunt for them; but they assumed, as Flosi had guessed they would, that the burners had ridden east, and failed to find them. It was evidently decided to wait until Flosi's band broke up and the members of it returned to their various homes, or at least came to visit their wives, when they could be dealt with separately. But Flosi had thought of this too, and he insisted that the band should stay together and ride home with him. This they did, and stayed with him for some months. It gives some idea of the size of Flosi's establishment that it could apparently take in and house and feed a hundred and twenty extra men for months. We are told that Flosi never spoke of the burning.

*   *   *   *

When the ruins of Njal's house were searched and men came to the spot where Njal had lain down they dug through a great heap of ashes and found the bull's hide shrivelled with the heat. But when they raised the hide the bodies of Njal and Bergthora and Kari's child were found unburnt beneath it, except for one of the boy's fingers, which he had stretched out from under the hide, and which was burnt off. The fact that the bodies were unburnt was thought to be 'a great token', though, of course, the fresh hide may well have protected them from the fire. The faces of Njal and Bergthora were also particularly calm and 'bright'.

They found the body of Skarphedinn hard up against the gable wall where the falling roof had pinned him. His legs were burnt off to the knees, but the rest of him was unburnt. 'He had bitten through his underlip, his eyes were wide open and not swollen or starting out of his head. He had driven his axe into the gable wall so hard that it had gone in up to the middle of the blade, and that was why it was not softened.' When they came to strip his body for burial they found marks on his shoulders and chest, branded in the shape of a cross, and it was thought that he must have burnt them on himself deliberately. From what we know of Skarphedinn such piety does not seem very likely, but there was a general desire on the part of the searchers to find as many near-miracles and 'tokens' as possible.

More moving to most of us is the fact that they also found the body of the old woman Saevuna, who had beaten the wicked stack of vetch and prophesied the use to which it would be put. She had been Bergthora's foster mother, and must have refused to go out with the other women.

THE AFTERMATH OF THE CRIME

Although Kari and a large band of supporters had ridden out to hunt for the burners immediately after the deed, it does not seem to have been felt possible to pursue them to the east once they had reached Flosi's home; and since the band carefully kept together throughout the winter, all Kari and his party could do was to organize for the maximum of support when the suit against the burners was brought at the ALTHING. Flosi was also busy seeking support, and did not hesitate to use bribes to get it, for he was a very rich man. The bribings and lobbyings and appeals for help before the THING were very similar to those that went on when Flosi was bringing his suit against the sons of Njal, but with one rather disreputable addition. Snorri the Priest, who seems to have been a wise but not particularly scrupulous person, had had a great respect and liking for Njal. As a priest, he was one of the officials of the ALTHING and partly responsible for its organization and conduct. Nevertheless, he secretly agreed with Kari's party that if a quarrel arose at the THING which ended in a fight, as all realized it might well do, he would post his men so that Flosi and his party could not escape, wait until Kari's party had killed as many of them as they could afford to pay for in blood fines, and then use his men to part them.

But by no means all the skulduggery was being carried on on one side, for the man who was advising Flosi, Eyjolf, put forward an idea similar in A. Cheever Loophole quality to the one that Mord had used on behalf of Njal's sons in the previous suit. It was that Flosi should hand over his priesthood to his brother and declare privately, but before witnesses, that he had joined a THING in the north. Kari's party, not knowing this, would bring their suit in the court which dealt with eastern problems, and it would then be possible to non-suit them for applying to the wrong court.

When the suit came to be heard it consisted almost entirely of this sort of legal quibbling, and once again, although the guilt of those charged was glaringly obvious, things reached a stage where not only did Kari's party seem likely to lose their suit but by some legalistic legerdemain they were in danger of being outlawed themselves.

Now there was no Njal to intervene on behalf of justice

and common sense. Kari's party, infuriated, attacked Flosi's party, and there was a pitched battle in which a number of men were killed and Flosi himself was wounded. Flosi and his band tried to get away, but Snorri the Priest, in accordance with his secret promise, was guarding the way of escape, and the battle went on for some time until Snorri, presumably having carefully reckoned up how many blood fines had been incurred, intervened to end it.

On the following day men were in a calmer mood. Hall of the Side, Flosi's father-in-law, who had played a pacific part in the previous suit between Flosi and Njal's sons, now came forward and suggested atonement. Kari at once refused to be party to any atonement, but the rest of his party agreed, except for Thorgeir, a kinsman of Skarphedinn; and Snorri the Priest went to work, doubtless helped by his previous calculations, to decide who owed what for killing whom.

A similar balance sheet was drawn up in the suit about the burning. Njal was to be atoned for with a triple fine (that is to say, six hundred ounces of silver, as had been paid for Hauskuld the Priest of Whiteness) and Bergthora, Grim, and Helgi were both to be paid for with double fines. The death of Skarphedinn was to be set off against that of Hauskuld, which we feel would have amused him. Kari, of course, refused atonement for the death of his son. Flosi and all the burners should go abroad into banishment for three years, under pain of being proclaimed outlaws. It is satisfactory to find that Gunnar Lambi's son and Grani Gunnar's son were banished for life.

These sentences of banishment were unavoidable, since the burning was an 'irredeemable crime' which could not be fully settled for money. It is a tribute to the general respect for Flosi that he was not outlawed but merely banished for three years, and given plenty of time to put his affairs in order before going. We do not know whether in all this complicated accountancy the money originally subscribed to atone the death of

Hauskuld the Priest was used, or, if so, how. Flosi refused to put in a counterclaim for his wound, and none of his followers were awarded anything for their injuries in the battle at the ALTHING, which caused some indignation amongst them. Apparently Snorri the Priest's approach was strictly one of whole life insurance, and not of sickness benefits. You were not entitled to any money unless you were actually dead.

Yet despite wounds, fines, and banishment, Flosi and the burners were still by no means out of the wood, since both Kari and Thorgeir Craggeir had refused atonement, which meant that they had reserved the right to take vengeance on the burners as and when they could. What this could mean was illustrated not long after Flosi had returned home from the THING. The sons of Sigfus had returned to his home with him, and now they asked to go away for two days to deal with some of their affairs. Flosi gave them leave, but warned them of the danger. Kari and Thorgeir Craggeir trailed them and came upon them when they were asleep. Scorning to kill sleeping men, Kari and Thorgeir woke them up, and then, though they were only two against fifteen, killed five of them and put the rest to flight.

Flosi therefore resolved to try to make peace with Thorgeir, with the object of isolating Kari, and an offer was made to him that no atonement should be asked for the killing of the sons of Sigfus, but that he should have an atonement for Njal and his sons. A similar offer was made to Kari, but he at once rejected it. Thorgeir hesitated to desert Kari, but Kari pressed him to accept the atonement on the grounds that they had now avenged the burning, and that all that was outstanding was revenge for the death of his son, which was his own affair. On this Thorgeir agreed to the atonement.

Even alone, however, Kari continued to harass the burners and before they went abroad in accordance with the terms of banishment he accounted for another six of them, showing mercy only to Kettle of the Mark, Njal's son-in-law. Then he pursued them to the Orkneys, where Flosi and some of the band had taken service with Earl Sigurd. On Christmas Day the Earl and some of his followers were drinking in the hall and Gunnar Lambi's son was asked to tell the story of the burning. As he was doing so, in 'an unfair and sneering way' Kari rushed in with his sword drawn and cut the head from his shoulders with a single blow. The earl would have had Kari seized and killed, but Flosi intervened, saying that Kari was in no atonement with him and his followers and 'only did what he had a right to do'. Flosi had the greatest admiration for Kari, and we know that he had always disliked and despised Gunnar Lambi's son.

It is interesting that if he were going to kill any of the burners in this reckless way Kari should not have chosen Flosi himself, and it seems likely that Flosi's admiration for him was reciprocated. After Flosi had finished his term of banishment he returned to Iceland, and Kari, returning also, was shipwrecked near Flosi's home. Without hesitation Kari went to Flosi and asked for, and was given, hospitality. After this there was a full reconciliation between them, and Kari married Flosi's niece, the same Hildigunna who had been the wife of Hauskuld the Priest of Whiteness.

On this rather trite note of 'happy ending' the Saga closes. It must be said that after the grand climax of the burning the story falls away both in interest and conviction and in vividness of telling. We begin to have an uncomfortable feeling that when the Norsemen discovered America they also discovered Hollywood. Kari was undoubtedly a great warrior, and he is in many ways a handsome, dashing, and attractive figure of the best Douglas Fairbanks, Senior, type. But he lacks the more subtle interest of the ashen-pale Skarphedinn, with his projecting front teeth, his quick tongue, and his ironic humour; just as his exploits in hunting down the sons of Sigfus lack the interest of what has gone before and become something of a dull formality. Perhaps by this stage the reader is tired of people being killed. I have never counted the actual number of killings in the Saga, but it must certainly total well over a hundred. It is pleasant enough to be told how Flosi and Kari eventually sat down together to drink as friends, and one wishes that Njal and Skarphedinn and Helgi and Grim and Haaskuld and Hauskuld the Priest of Whiteness, and possibly even Thrain, could have been with them. But unfortunately they were all dead. Perhaps, after all, it is as well that they could not be there. Probably there would only have been another quarrel.

Yet the Saga recovers itself for a moment in almost its last lines when we have our final glimpse of Flosi as an old man. 'Men say that the end of Flosi's life was that he fared abroad, when he had grown old, to seek for timber to build him a hall. He was in Norway that winter, but the next summer he sailed late; and men told him that his ship was not seaworthy. Flosi said she was quite good enough for an old and death-doomed man, and bore his goods on shipboard, and put out to sea. But of that ship no tidings were ever heard.'

*   *   *   *

A friend of mine whose business it is to enquire into airplane accidents once complained that people always wanted to know the *reason* for the accident; and it was practically always impossible to give them a single reason, or, indeed, even the principal reason. In almost all airplane accidents there were a whole series of small factors, not one of which would have brought about the accident by itself. Yet without any one of them it would not have happened. The way in which these comparatively small factors gradually added and fitted together to make a fatal situation struck him as almost uncanny.

The same is true of the tragedy of Burnt Njal. The length of the chain of events, and the way in which each link added to the chain moves us a little nearer to the final tragedy of the burning, almost seems to justify the fatalism of the Norsemen, 'What is doomed to be, will be', and men, as both the Greeks and Lear thought, are but the toys of the gods and of fate.

But if the fates were at work to destroy Njal and his sons

they certainly carried out their work through some very normal and human agencies. The type of crime which is carried out by psychopaths or grossly maladjusted persons has only a rare interest, of the sort we might feel in a man with two heads or a monstrously fat lady at a fair. They have little connection with ordinary life we as know it. But the crimes in the story of Njal are usually carried out for reasons which we can fully understand, even if we do not approve of them. None of the principal characters is what we should usually regard as 'a criminal type', any more than Othello is; and most of them, like Othello, have many heroic qualities. Yet all of them (with the possible exception of the all-too-perfect Kari) have those 'heroic flaws' in character which have always been the sources of the greatest tragedies.

Thus Njal himself, though wise, statesmen-like, and possessed of much foresight—a man in every way in advance of his time—could be both tactless and unrealistic in his dealings with people whose temperaments were very different from his own. In his passionate desire for peace he seems to have forgotten that there were others who valued it considerably less highly than he did. Like Mr. Chamberlain in dealing with Hitler, he did not realize that a policy of appeasement will not work with people who simply do not want to be appeased.

The chief amongst these were his own sons. They were young, vigorous men and outstanding warriors, in a day when the warrior was the type of man most generally admired. Fighting was their business, their hobby, and their pride, and in a world as Njal would have had it they would have been miserably under-employed. In modern terms they were warmongers. They took the sword, and eventually perished by it, as they would have wished; for if they may not have gone to the heaven of their new Christian faith they would certainly have gone to the Valhalla of their old one. Paradoxically, the young sons were far more old-fashioned than their elderly father.

Perhaps the most interesting character is Flosi. If Njal was the left-wing intellectual, and his sons were old-fashioned Tories, or even Fascists, Flosi was in a position somewhere left of centre—always the most difficult of positions for a man of serious mind. At the outset Flosi was prepared, and indeed anxious, to follow the rule of law, and was even prepared to put up with criticism and insult to do so. But Flosi was a practical man rather than an intellectual like Njal, and when, through defects in its machinery, the rule of law failed him he had no real roots of faith to sustain him and felt that he had no alternative but to return to the old ways. The parallel with the action of Britain and France over Suez a thousand years later is terrifyingly clear. Flosi's good intentions foundered on impatience. Because the machinery of law was not yet working properly, then it must be discarded, and what he knew was morally wrong must nevertheless be done in order to get immediate results. And so a noble and decent man takes his followers to church and then goes and commits a horrible, brutal, and unsuccessful crime, and lives the rest of his life wondering whether he was right or wrong, since both the new methods and the old seemed to have failed him.

This confusion in the mind of Flosi, the well-meaning practical man, is not only a reflection of the confused state of society in his own day but of the standard problems of any society throughout history, including our own. In Flosi's time Europe was only just emerging from the Dark Ages, and it was groping for something to replace what had been lost with the disappearance of Greece and the Roman Empire. The evolution of law and of a social structure is a matter of trial and error. The Icelandic community had not been established long, and the surprising thing is not that they put so much trust in violence but that there were so many men like Njal and Hall of the Side and Kettle of the Mark who saw the possibilities of the rule of law. The process of trial and error is still going on. Like Flosi, nations today are restrained from violence by two things —their principles and their fear of the consequences. But once Flosi lost faith in the principles he had supported, his fear of the consequences alone was not enough to restrain him. The moral need not be laboured.

The main difference between our own problems and those of the Icelanders is one of size rather than one of kind—the unit was the family rather than the nation. Yet even here the problems created by separate groups with separate loyalties are essentially the same. 'My country right or wrong' is only 'My family right or wrong' writ larger, and therefore liable to be destructive on a larger scale. The intense family loyalty of the Icelanders meant that men of intelligence did not feel themselves free to act according to their own convictions, if such actions were contrary to the family interests and the family honour. Thus Njal, the left-wing intellectual, has to support his rugger-tough old-fashioned sons simply because they are his sons. Kettle of the Mark, a very reasonable and pacific man, has to be present at the burning because he was one of the sons of Sigfus. Flosi had to take up the blood feud because the murdered man was the husband of his niece; and Hall of the Side, another of the pacifist intellectuals, has to support Flosi because he is his son-in-law. We feel that had the unit been the nation rather than the family, then Njal, Hall, and Kettle, and possibly Flosi, could have formed a united party against those like Njal's sons and Thrain, who refused to accept the rule of law.

To the extent that it enables men of goodwill to act together the larger unit is certainly an improvement on the smaller one. But the larger unit also enables the stupid, reactionary, and the straightforward criminals to act together, and so ensure that if anything goes wrong the disaster is on a larger scale. The band that Flosi drew together was an exceptionally large one by Icelandic standards, and Flosi almost certainly felt in a vague way that what he was carrying out was a sort of police action. But quite apart from the goodwill or otherwise of its members, the band represented only a sectional interest, and all it managed to do in the end was to turn what had otherwise been a comparatively small-scale family quarrel into something which

brought about a pitched battle at the ALTHING. 'Police action'
by sectional interests nearly had the same result over Suez,
and even in the Congo.

The answer to the problem, of course, is childishly simple
to state and fantastically difficult to implement. Assuming
that there are more men of goodwill than men of illwill, what
stands between us and a reasonable society is group loyalty,
which, however huge the groups concerned, still prevents all the
men of goodwill from acting together. The Icelanders sailed
away from Norway and King Harald Fairhair because of a
passionate desire to retain their independence—for each man
to be cock on his own dunghill, and to live his own life with his
own family, without interferences from people who were 'not
of his blood'. Independence and loyalty to one's blood are
much admired qualities. But a thousand years later the desire
of millions of Russians, Americans, Chinese, Indians, and even
Englishmen, to live their own lives in their own way without
interference from people who are not of their blood leaves the
Icelanders' problem multiplied by many millions but still un-
solved. We can see now what Flosi should have done when the
ALTHING proved impotent to give him justice. He should have
accepted the atonement offered by Njal, that other man of
goodwill, and thereafter have worked for an ALTHING which
could have implemented the ideas they both believed in. But
the practical, impatient man lost his temper, and rode away
and abandoned his new-found principles, and burnt up the
good with the bad in an 'irredeemable crime'. It is not the
criminal that we have to fear. It is the well-meaning but
impatient Flosi, with no really deep-rooted belief in the im-
provability of society. If he arises in our own world, his power,
multiplied many millionfold but his problem basically the same,
he will probably still lead his followers to church before he sets
out for Bergthorsknoll, in a desperate effort to prove that he
is committing a crime on principle. But this time the burning
house will fall in on something more than Njal and his family.

C. S. FORESTER

William Joyce

'MR. ATTORNEY and Mr. Slade, I shall direct the jury on Count 3 that on August 24th, 1939, when the passport was applied for, the prisoner, beyond the shadow of a doubt, owed allegiance to the Crown of this country, and that on the evidence given, if they accept it, nothing happened at the material time thereafter to put an end to the allegiance that he then owed.'

Those were the first words that Mr. Justice Tucker spoke when the court reopened after an adjournment, during which the judge had been weighing the submissions put forward by the prosecution and the defence in the trial of William Joyce. The speech made it quite certain that William Joyce would be condemned to death for treason. The last eighteen words were all that mattered. None had denied that on August 24th, 1939, Joyce owed allegiance to the Crown of England; admittedly, he had been resident in England at that date, and by the mere fact of residence he owed that allegiance—'local allegiance'— like any other alien, to the government of the country in which he was living. Mr. Justice Tucker now stated that Joyce, an alien, could be guilty of treason against England even after he had changed his residence and had gone to live in Germany. That meant, quite obviously, that he would be found guilty, for none could deny that he had adhered to the King's enemies from the moment of the declaration of war, even though the evidence given at the trial regarding that adherence during the opening months was sketchy in the extreme, as his defending counsel pointed out. Joyce had on August 24th, 1939, applied for, and received, a renewal of his British passport

61

until July 1940, and Mr. Justice Tucker had now ruled that in consequence until July 1st, 1940, Joyce owed allegiance to the British Crown. It did not matter that the passport had been fraudulently obtained; it did not matter that no evidence was put forward to show that Joyce had made any use at all of the fatal document. The passport had been issued and renewed; until it expired Joyce, an American citizen, owed allegiance to King George VI and he could not divest himself of that allegiance even by leaving England to live in Germany.

That was the law, as Mr. Justice Tucker stated it; in the Court of Appeal his finding was unanimously upheld; in the House of Lords four law lords out of five upheld it, so that altogether there were eight learned opinions to one regarding this point of law. In consequence William Joyce—Lord Haw-Haw—was found guilty of treason and hanged; it was the date written in his passport that, at least to all appearances, brought about his death. Presumably if a different date had been written there he would have been found not guilty, for example if that passport had happened to be valid up to, say, September 1st, 1939, instead of July 1st, 1940, and Joyce had gone to Germany without renewing it. There is nothing wild about that possibility, and there are other possibilities that excite specula-tion as well. Joyce undoubtedly went to Germany against the wishes of the police who would have prevented his leaving the country; it is not known by what means he achieved this, but it is at least possible that he might have been equally successful if he had carried an out-of-date passport. Or he might have made use of the passport of a friend or an accomplice—but that might not have saved his life later, for a borrowed or stolen passport might be presumed to impose a duty of allegience in the same way as one fraudulently obtained. Joyce might conceivably, in the brief interval between his arrival in Germany and the declaration of war, have naturalized himself as a German—as indeed he did a year later—without the fact coming to the knowledge of the British authorities. In that case no charge of treason could have been brought against him. In the case of William Joyce, first and last Lord Haw-Haw, there was only the faintest dividing line between his being formally a traitor or formally an honest and open enemy of England; it was a line drawn by ritual, by convention, it might be said. He was the wrong side of it and he suffered death, not having foreseen, or allowed for, all the necessary formalities.

So much for the formal side of this curious case, at least for the present. In actual truth, how much of a traitor was he? Truth is notoriously hard to establish. Did he believe himself to be an Englishman fighting on a matter of principle against his king and country? He tried to give every impression that he did so believe. Yet he could hardly have done anything else. If he had prefaced his famous broadcasts with the statement that he was an American, a neutral, intervening in the struggle between the British and the German ideologies, he would never have been listened to; his speeches would have lost all point. The whole of the British public, and not merely a part of it, would have laughed at him while despising him. Furthermore, when he made his statement after his arrest, as he lay in his hopsital bed recovering from the flesh wound he had received, his opening words revealed the secret of his birth. He declared, what was the truth, that he was American-born and that he understood his parents at his birth were American citizens. If that were what he understood then he had always known—or at least strongly suspected—that he was legally an American citizen and he took the very first opportunity after his arrest to say so. It was in the forefront of his mind as he planned his carefully reasoned statement. Perhaps he merely wanted to deprive his British captors of the satisfaction of making the discovery for themselves; perhaps he was relying upon it to save his life—perhaps the knowledge had been at the back of his mind to reassure him during the dark days when Germany was going down to defeat.

He must have always have been aware of it. At the trial his brother Quentin swore (and there is every reason to believe his evidence) that he himself had been let into the secret in 1927 or 1928, when he was ten or eleven years old. William Joyce by that time was twenty-one or twenty-two; we can be quite sure that for many years before that he had been aware that legally he was an American. His motive for concealing the fact will become apparent later in this essay.

He must have known he was legally an American when at the age of sixteen he wrote his fulsome letter to the University of London authorities applying for admission to the Officers' Training Corps. 'I am in no way connected with the United States of America, against which, as against all other nations, I am prepared to draw the sword in British interests.' The flamboyant style can be excused in a boy of sixteen; the lie may perhaps be explained. He was quite well aware, when he joined the British Fascists at the age of seventeen, that technically he was an American, and that technically he should be waving the Stars and Stripes instead of the Union Jack which the fascists displayed so freely. He knew he was an American while he spoke and worked for the Conservative party, and while he worked for Sir Oswald Mosley and the British Union of Fascists; he knew it when he stood for Shoreditch in the municipal elections of 1937, even though this involved making a statutory declaration that he was a British subject and rendered him liable to fine and imprisonment should the truth be discovered. He knew it while he spouted the particular kind of patriotism favoured by the Fascists, and he knew it when he made his last journey to Germany and when he first spoke into a microphone those famous words 'Germany calling'.

In this case how much of a traitor was he? He had left America at the age of three and could have no American memories. His father had been strongly Conservative and of Imperialist ideals. He must have always thought of himself as an Englishman, despite the nagging and disturbing certainty that he was not, and he could reassure himself with the knowledge that Napoleon, the patriotic Frenchman, had been born a Corsican, and Hitler, the patriotic German, had been born an Austrian. He may have thought that the Fascist ideals and the Fascist plans for altering the British constitution would lead to a better England. He may have acted throughout from the purest idealism; it may be said cynically that the reformer who takes up arms to effect a revolution is a traitor only if he fails. He may well have believed—as his statement declared— that the Nazi system should be applied to England for her own good; he may have seen no objection to Hitler himself enforcing that system in England. If all this is true Joyce was a desperately unlucky martyr in a wrong-headed cause. Was it true?

Joyce was a man of considerable education; he held an honours degree in English and history. If he believed all the nonsense he talked he must have been a fool. If, after his visits to Germany under the Nazi regime before the war, he believed there was any merit in Nazi methods he must have been mentally blind. But if he believed none of this and still went on acting as he did then he must have been a self-seeker of the deepest dye, aiming solely at making a position for himself in the world at any cost whatever to others. That means he was guilty of the worst kind of treachery, the blackest possible kind, which in the opinion of the world merits nothing less than hanging—even if before the hanging takes place there must be a legal enquiry into the dating of a passport.

So further examination of his character and antecedents is necessary. Without doubt he was a man of restless ambition, dissatisfied with his present position. He chafed under the handicap with which he was burdened. He was a little man of slightly comic appearance. The dreadful scar that swept across his right cheek from ear to mouth (no one knows exactly how he acquired it) was not so much impressive as merely grotesque. His birth emphatically conferred upon him no social position; by the time he reached his teens his father had sunk down the social scale and was merely a grocer in Clapham. Joyce himself was never able to acquire the manner and the accent which would enable him to pass as a member of the privileged classes, nor, on the other hand, was he blessed with the personality or the indifference which frequently in English society enables a self-made man to rise superior to his handicaps. He could be good company, he could be witty and forceful in speech, and yet he could never contrive to be accepted at the value he set on himself—he was not gifted in the way Hitler was.

Most of the people with whom he found himself associating were quite incapable ever of taking an honours degree at London University and yet they paid him no deference. He was active, ingenious, resolute, and yet no golden prizes and certainly no adulation came his way, even though he held high office in Sir Oswald Mosley's Fascist organization and proved himself an efficient manager of the dangerous but infantile hobble-de-hoys of whom he had to make use. He was Deputy Leader and Director of Propaganda—the British Hess and the British Goebbels rolled into one—but that did not suffice, for he was incapable of according Mosley the devotion—quite genuine—which Hitler inspired in these lieutenants, and Mosley was incapable of inspiring it. There was an absurd disagreement over policy. Mosley, with his slogan of 'Mind Britain's Business', advocated allowing the dictators a free hand in Europe, for he had enough political acumen to realize that to advocate more rigorous alliance with Hitler would not help to popularize his movement. Joyce, on the other hand, was all for the closest possible association with the dictators; he wished for an international Fascism, partly, it appears, because he really believed that Hitler was a great organizer inspired by great ideas. The inevitable split between Mosley and Joyce received a good deal of attention in the British Press; the announcement was made that Mosley had dismissed Joyce from all his offices, and in the same month Joyce was organizing the British National Socialist League as a rival to the British Union of Fascists. It never achieved a membership one-tenth as numerous, despite all Joyce's efforts.

While Joyce had been associated with the British Union of Fascists a technique had been devised—possibly or probably by Joyce himself—to cause disturbances that would attract the attention of Press and public while enabling the instigators to pose as public-spirited martyrs defending the privilege of free speech. A meeting would be announced for some future date, and then every provocation that could be thought of would be offered to the public that was invited to attend. There were posters that both advocated violence and challenged it; there were parades, uniforms, a campaign of muttered threats. On the day of the meeting the town would be filled with insolent and swaggering young blackguards who served the double purpose of infuriating the public and of providing an audience —an applauding audience—when at last the meeting took place.

Then there would be fiery nonsense from the platform, in which the public was recommended to abandon all their hard-won liberties and confer a dictatorship on Sir Oswald to enable him to persecute the Jews, and when the speeches were ended the blackguards marched out to meet and provoke the waiting crowd. Little additional provocation was necessary; representatives of counter-organizations were there, not so well disciplined and not so cunningly commanded, besides the indignant members of the general public. Loud remarks by one Fascist to another; gibes and insults; it was inevitable that words should be answered by blows. That meant a riot, in which the well-organized Fascists had the advantage of unity and discipline which enabled them to indulge their taste for violence with small danger to themselves. People were beaten unconscious, noses were broken and teeth knocked out and ribs kicked in, but it was not the Fascists who had struck the first blow. They were only defending themselves, and that was what the courts of justice necessarily decided in the subsequent trials. Mosley himself, as well as Joyce, was acquitted— quite in accordance with the evidence—on a charge of riotous assembly at Worthing.

As Leader of the National Socialist League Joyce practised this technique over and over again. Twice he was tried for assault in the London courts and twice he was acquitted; the police chafed against their helplessness and could do nothing more. Joyce had profited by his study of history. He knew how both Louis Napoleon and Hitler had commanded public attention by undergoing trials in public courts, and he knew very well how Hitler had risen to power within the framework of the law after a disastrous use of open violence.

In Joyce's own case, however, the irritation of the police authorities was specially dangerous. There was the question of his birth. If ever the police were to discover that legally he was an American citizen he could be in no doubt as to his fate. He certainly would not be prosecuted for failing to register as an alien, or for making a false declaration in his application for his passport, or for standing for a seat on a borough council. He would be shipped off to America instantly and ignominiously, amid sighs of relief from all concerned, and the immigration authorities would see to it that he would never again set foot in this England which he so often declared he loved—possibly with truth.

That was the shadow that hung over him; it was allied to the shadow that hung over his father. For both he and his father had been involved in the troubles associated with the movement for Irish independence. Joyce was three years old when his parents returned with him from America to Ireland; he was ten when the Dublin rebellion took place; he was fifteen when independence was finally granted. Yet he declared that, young though he was, he had taken part on the British side— the losing side—in the war for independence. 'I have served with the irregular forces of the Crown in an intelligence capacity against the Irish guerillas', which can only mean that as a mere child he acted as spy and informer for one faction against another, perhaps from the highest motives. At any rate, if there was any truth in the story at all, his most formative years had been spent in an atmosphere of hatred and fear, treachery and murder.

His father, Michael Joyce, had most certainly been deeply

involved. He was described by a sergeant of the Royal Irish Constabulary in 1917 as 'one of the most respectable, law-abiding, and loyal men in this locality' and in 1917 that meant a great deal more than those simple words might imply. A mere neutral in the struggle for independence was not re-garded as 'loyal' in the eyes of the Royal Irish Constabulary, and subsequent events prove that Michael Joyce must have been an active agent working for the Crown forces. His leaving Ireland as soon as independence was granted might not be specially significant—a certain number of other loyalists emigrated as well—but it is certainly significant that the 'ex-tensive house property' which the police had reported him to possess had dwindled in value so that he reappears in a small grocer's shop in Clapham; a man regarded as a traitor by the new regime in Ireland would not be able to sell his houses for anything approaching their full value.

Then there was all the secrecy. Michael Joyce did his best not to attract public notice. He made no attempt to re-naturalize as British, even though it would not have been a difficult or complicated process—but it would have involved statutory notices in the newspapers, giving his name and address, and the Irish memory was long and the Irish hatred for treachery was intense. The obscure grocer in Clapham might expect to escape notice only as long as he called no attention to himself. Hence the secrecy, the burning of documents that Quentin Joyce described, and Michael Joyce's determination to go all his life as a stateless person (he had lost his acquired American nationality by failing to register) unnoticed by anyone—in which he actually succeeded.

Perhaps William Joyce's life was also in danger; perhaps Irish fanatics might have taken vengeance on a child who had acted 'in an intelligence capacity'. It does not seem likely now but may well have seemed likely then. By 1923, less than two years after his return (or his flight) to England, William Joyce was a member of the British Fascists, and the reasons why he should never admit that he was an American citizen became steadily more and more numerous. He was saddled with the secret and could not unburden himself until he became one of Hitler's subjects in 1940. It must have been a powerful factor in making him the disturbed individual that he undoubtedly was.

Yet during his troubled youth he displayed considerable mental capacity. Six months after his entrance—or flight—into England he passed the University of London matriculation; he was sixteen, the usual age, so that the Irish troubles had not prevented him from acquiring a basic education. He failed at the intermediate stage in his attempt to take a degree in science, but, changing over to English and history, he took his degree with honours when he was twenty-one—something more than a modest achievement.

He was already supporting himself, as a teacher on the staff of a tutorial college, and had no difficulty in retaining his employers' regard. Even before he took his degree—within a week of his coming of age, in fact—he married; it may be significant, it may have added to his troubles, that the marriage took place in a register office although he was a Catholic. However disturbed he may have been, mentally or spiritually, those disturbances did nothing to moderate his activities—they may have goaded him on. He taught for a living, supporting himself and his wife and the two daughters, who were the fruit of the marriage, and meanwhile he did one year's post-graduate work in philology and two years' work in psychology while working and speaking for the Conservative Party.

The marriage ended in divorce when he was thirty; even at its easiest and simplest divorce is a disturbing experience, and to a man brought up as a Catholic, the father of two children, it may have been very disturbing. Certainly it added a fresh burden, a new worry, from which he had been singularly free until then, for he married again and now had not only to support his present wife but he had to contribute to the support of his children and his first wife, all this at the moment when he was breaking with Mosley—there was gossip to the effect that the real cause of the break was Mosley's discovery that Joyce had been embezzling the funds of the British Union of Fascists.

Nevertheless it was now that Joyce moved to a more expensive home, in Onslow Gardens, South Kensington, where he entertained extensively and noisily; the doctor who lived on the floor below, who was his landlord, was frequently disconcerted by the strange guests who arrived, while the doctor's wife felt sorry for Mrs. Joyce, who was a willing and loving slave to her eccentric and exacting husband. It may be noticed here that both the doctor and his wife experienced the dual reaction to Joyce's personality, of liking combined with repulsion, that many other people reported as their experience. His incredible vulgarity seemed to be a means of self-assertion, of attracting notice, and to have developed as a reaction against the smoother manners he had never been able to adopt; he could, on occasions, reveal a different self; cultured, witty, and even gentle.

There were numerous visitors to the flat in Onslow Gardens. Joyce had a car and even in the 1930s cars cost money. He had offices in London and a shop in Bristol, and he issued a newspaper. It is beyond belief that *The Helmsman* brought in, by sales and advertising, one-tenth of the cost of production. Nor could the profits from sales in the shop in Bristol, which sold daggers and knuckle-dusters and similar equipment for rioters, have gone far towards paying the rent. The British National Socialist League had only the smallest membership; Joyce had no wealthy backers in England, and although he worked desperately hard speaking in public (often several times in a day), writing inflammatory articles, getting himself arrested and acquitted, sending out thousands of letters, he was never able to build up more than a small following, and his audiences mostly came from the poorer strata of society.

Joyce was still teaching, despite all these other activities (it should be remembered that his teaching was conducted through the post, so that he never had to go to work at regular hours), but his earnings could not possibly cover his outgoings. He was spending thousands and thousands of pounds every year more than he received from the enterprises already listed, and that money came from Germany, from Hitler, through Hitler's chief of propaganda, Goebbels. These were the years 1937, 1938, 1939. There was the Anschluss with Austria to be explained. There was the agitation about the Sudeten Deutsch to be justified. There was the agreement at Munich to be excused, then the final absorption of Czechoslovakia. Then a move had to be made to prepare British public opinion for the demands to be made on Poland.

The Nazi government was glad to spare some of its precious foreign exchange, even with German rearmament making vast demands upon it, if in return they could hope to keep the British government subservient or blind. They were very willing to give Joyce thousands of pounds for his help. Even in the muddle-headed England of that day, with its terrible memories of the Somme and Passchendaele, there were very few people willing to accept Nazi money and work in furtherance of Nazi aims. Joyce was not a very effective instrument, but he was better than none at all.

How much of a traitor was he? Legally, even if he were an Englishman by birth, he was guilty of no crime. There was no statute on the books, there was nothing in Common Law, to prevent someone in England from receiving money from a foreign power and in exchange advocating a political programme. Joyce may well have been perfectly sincere in his belief that England should, for her own good, act in concert with Hitler or at least refrain from opposition. This was also Hitler's passionate desire. Even much later, after the fall of France, he addressed the world—Germans, neutrals, and enemies alike—in a famous speech in which he offered peace to England on speciously reasonable terms. The Nazi propaganda department was well aware of this cardinal factor in Hitler's policy, however brief might be the friendship he desired, and whatever he planned for the future after its termination. Goebbels must have been glad to find someone in England who

would help; he must have been glad, in his conferences with
Hitler, to be able to produce a copy of *The Helmsman*, and the
reports in English newspapers of Joyce's behaviour, as proofs
that Nazi money was being well spent under his supervision.
And Joyce may have been glad to be granted the opportunity
to forward the aims of Hitler, who was doing his inspired best
to make a better world. He may have been glad; he may have
thought in this way; he may have thought that the Jews
exerted a sinister influence and should be persecuted in consequence; he certainly believed, along with a majority of
people, that the Russian government was desirous of extending
its influence and doctrine at the expense of the West and should
be restrained, if not overthrown.

It is hard to believe in the sincerity of a wrong-headed person,
even if there is a grain or two of sense among the nonsense.
A man who advocates a revolutionary policy, one clearly
opposed to common sense or to accepted doctrine, is bound to
be suspect, and the more vehement his advocacy, the stronger
grows the suspicion that his motives are sinister. Joyce, as has
been pointed out before, may well have been merely self-seeking, desirous of becoming an important figure in the world
without regard to morality; but the possibility must not be
overlooked that he may have been the martyr he claimed to be,
sincere even though misguided. Likely enough, the truth may
lie between those two extremes. His belief in Nazi doctrines
may have been subconsciously strengthened by the thought
that their success would elevate him in the world; the possibility that England might be humiliated may have held some
concealed attraction for a man who had himself been humiliated often enough; there was something so convenient that it
might be fore-ordained about the fact that the Nazis should
offer him money in exchange for his willing help at a time when
he was in financial straits.

That passport; he had applied for it in July 1933, as soon as
Hitler had gained power, and it had taken him to Germany, to
the vast satisfaction of the Nuremberg rallies, to the lavish

hospitality of the propaganda department, to see with his own eyes how magnificently the successful revolutionary would live. It expired in 1938, the year of Munich—and in the month of Munich he applied for its renewal. For three months he had allowed it to lapse; now he asked for it to be renewed for a single year. It was no harder to obtain a renewal for five years than for one; the difference in the fee was no more than a few shillings. It is a curious point which might be highly significant. It might indicate that Joyce was convinced that he would only need the passport for a short time, that before a year was out the passport would have no value or no meaning. It seems quite certain that by arrangement with his German paymasters he was planning to go to Germany before war should break out over the Sudeten question.

But the crisis passed, and war was postponed, and Joyce remained in England to continue his efforts on behalf of the Hitler government. Unexplainably he changed his residence, moving, in July 1939, to a much cheaper and less attractive flat in Earls Court, but he lived there only two months. On August 24th the episode with the passport was repeated; once more it had been allowed to expire (the renewal had been dated back to July 1st, 1938) and once more he applied for a renewal for a year. Perhaps it was for the same psychological reasons, because of some feeling of impermanence, of impending change. The crisis with regard to Hitler's demands upon Poland was growing more and more intense. War was likely, war was almost certain, and Joyce was wanted in Germany if war should come. Probably he very much wanted to go; possibly he thought it was his duty to go. Certainly if war were to come he would cease to draw any money from the German government—he would be faced with instant poverty. That could be an important factor in the plans of anybody; more important in the plans of a mercenary. He was only thirty-three; in the event of war he could expect, if he stayed, to be conscripted into the British army and compelled to fight against his German friends and the Nazi system; that was a consideration that

might influence mercenary or fanatic alike. And he might think
—if he really believed in all he said, he must have been certain
—that by going to Germany he would be joining the winning
side.

So he walked into the passport office, filled in his application form, and walked out again with the renewed passport
that was going to hang him. That was the moment when the
pact between Germany and Russia was announced, when it
should have become apparent even to the blindest devotee that
Hitler had no objective, no ideal, except his own aggrandizement. No patriotic Englishman, however wrong-headed, no
one with any regard for the good of the world, could possibly
(it might be thought) have ever again have lifted a finger to
help Hitler. Joyce went to Germany to give all the help he
could. His wife went with him—she was devoted to him even
though he did not treat her as kindly as he might have done
and although quarrels were frequent.

The fact that he took his wife had a curious repercussion at
his trial, for it was part of the complicated law of treason that
an alien, resident in England, would still owe allegiance to the
British Crown if he were to go abroad and leave his family and
effects behind him, whether he held a British passport or not.
Joyce left his effects—such as they were—but he took his wife,
and thereby (quite inadvertently, one can be sure) spiked in
advance the most effective gun that the prosecution could
have used against him at his trial six years later. It may as well
be told at this point that the unfortunate woman could not be
tried for treason herself because of the presumption in law
that a wife in her husband's presence is under her husband's
influence; but at the same time the law held that she was a
German citizen in consequence of her husband's (perfectly
legal) naturalization in 1940, so that, having been brought to
England in 1945, she was deported back again and dumped,
willy-nilly, into the starving and chaotic Germany that existed
after the war; for her naturalization, while America was still
at peace with Germany, was not a treasonable act by an

American citizen—her marriage had made her such by English law, although not by American law. There were other legal complexities about her case as well, but surely enough have been mentioned in this short list.

The Joyces left England despite police precautions. William Joyce had been charged with a minor motoring offence for the express purpose of providing an excuse to keep him in the country, but the pair slipped through—no one knows how. Someone was careless, or possibly someone was treacherous, or, just barely possibly, the German government provided secret means of transportation for them. The prosecution at the trial could bring forward no evidence on this point at all. All that could be shown was that on August 27th, in London, Joyce publicly announced the dissolution of his National Socialist League (it would be interesting to know the motive behind that action) and that on September 18th he signed a contract in Berlin with a German radio company. Joyce might have embarrassed the prosecution at his trial considerably if he had been able to produce evidence that he had escaped from England without using his passport at all—he might even have gone into the witness-box and sworn that he had left the passport at home and had crossed the North Sea in a German fishing-boat or even a German sumarine. It would not have saved him, but it would have occasioned extreme embarrassment.

So now he was with his German friends and ready to open his campaign to induce England to drop out of the war, or to terrorize her into doing so. Soon he was speaking on the German radio, and for the first time English people heard that famous voice echoing from their loudspeakers. That famous voice; it provoked the most violent reaction in all that heard it. It was coarse and yet flexible; it could instil fear or it could arouse hatred. It was not quite an English voice; it was not quite the voice of a member of the upper classes. There was a hint of Irish about it and there was a hint of Cockney. It was a rabble-rouser's voice. An inspired actor, playing the part of one of the swaggering blackguards outside a Mosley meeting, might have spoken his lines in that same voice. There was a coarse quality about the timbre of it that caught the attention and stayed in the memory. It was instantly recognized by people who had heard Joyce speaking in public before the war—the first broadcasts had hardly been heard before identifications began to pour in to the British police.

Bearing all this in mind, one wonders why Joyce had not succeeded in gathering a large following while he was speaking in public in England. The explanation lies in his insignificant and grotesque appearance. No one seeing him while hearing him could possibly take him seriously, but his disembodied voice was a powerful instrument—it may have been well that before the war Joyce had never had the opportunity of addressing the public on the wireless. The United States of America has provided more than one example of rabble-rousing by radio.

The use Joyce made of this remarkable weapon, however, demonstrated his own coarse tendencies. There was no one else in the world who could gloat with the same gusto as he displayed. His hatred, his sham reasonableness, his pseudo-patriotism were all larger than life. He dragged out his sentences and he wrung every drop of emotion out of his individual words in a way that can only be compared with the speeches of the villains in the melodramas of the last century. It could hardly be that he was addressing himself to that kind of audience; the tendency was inherent in his nature.

Moreover, the early broadcasts were not very effective owing to their wild content. Very few people could have believed him when in October 1939 he announced that Folkestone and Dover were in ruins; it was too easy to check on his statements. Internal evidence seems to show that his early speeches were written for him and that he had to read them into the microphone whether he approved of them or not. The German government could not be quite sure yet that he was not a British agent cunningly planted on them by the British: besides, in Goebbels's propaganda office—as in every propaganda office—there must have been many people who believed themselves capable of composing good propaganda and were anxious to try their hands at it.

Later on he did better (or worse) when he had won more of his employers' confidence and had more facts to work on. When he was discussing British shipping losses it was astonishing how effectively he could enunciate such a prosaic phrase as 'gross registered tons'. Of course he would exult over the occupation of Norway and the fall of France.

When the air raids began he would exaggerate the damage done with little chance of being found out, and it was easier still to threaten worse. The conquest of Norway under the nose of the Royal Navy made his promises of the future invasion of England seem not so wild after all. The wholesale internment of possible traitors in England seemed to lend substance to his hints that a powerful pro-German party in England was only awaiting the right moment to declare itself. Where communication was unusually slow and difficult—as it was in England—and where a severe censorship was in force it was easy for gossip and rumour to spread, and it was easy for him to supply material.

Yet, as events turned out, he was never actually dangerous, and the most important factor in rendering him harmless was the nickname conferred upon him in an inspired moment by Mr. Jonah Barrington of the *Daily Express*, to whom his country still owes a debt of gratitude. From the moment Joyce became Lord Haw-Haw (the name was taken up instantly all over the country) much of his influence was nullified. Joyce was endeavouring to inspire fear; had that remarkable voice of his remained unlabelled—had it continued as a mysterious and powerful emanation from the unknown—he might have had more success. But it was far less likely that anyone should fear Lord Haw-Haw, whose comic name exactly fitted, and called attention to, the odder qualities of his accent.

Events themselves took much of the sting out of what he had to say. He had prophesied invasion, and the months rolled by and invasion became less and less likely. With ill-founded optimism he had declared that Italy would remain a firm ally of Germany, and six weeks after he uttered those words Mussolini had fallen and the new government of Italy declared for the Allies. He predicted Hitler's triumphant entry into Moscow, and Rommel's entry into Alexandria, and time soon revealed the worthlessness of his prophecies. The prophet of doom was shown to be a false prophet. Most of the success he achieved was not the result of his own efforts but of the wild gossip that was spread by thoughtless and irresponsible English people; the stories that went round about his amazing information—tales about his having remarked about the inaccuracies of English church clocks and having given detailed descriptions of recent bomb damage—were entirely without foundation. Examination of the recordings of his speeches shows that he never said these things at all.

Perhaps, too, he was not a very good propagandist. He could never speak without reference to the Jews; the British public had seen the thousands of Jews who had escaped from the Continent, and found it hard to believe that those wretched refugees could endanger the stability of the world, while British tolerance puzzled over Nazi hatred and fear and doubted the sanity of a party that could feel these emotions. He extolled the beneficent tyranny of Hitler; England remembered the massacres and knew something about the internment camps. He had nothing but praise for Hitler's foreign policy; England remembered the years of anxiety and turmoil which that policy had occasioned.

When all is said and done, his lack of success was basically due to the loyalty and determination of the British public. The detailed enquiries by the British authorities reveal that he won his largest audiences during the opening months of the war, during the period of the 'phony war' when there was little news in the papers and a puzzled public was trying to explain this inactivity to itself. When the crisis came, when England was in deadly danger, the British public closed its ranks and presented a united front that Joyce could never penetrate, and fewer and fewer people listened to what he had to say.

Indeed, it is hard to resist the conclusion that propaganda during the period 1939–45 was not as effective a weapon as people expected or feared or hoped. Joyce was on the losing side; his difficulties grew greater and greater, and it is likely that he was hampered by the stupidity and prejudices of his employers. But it is difficult to discover any notable success achieved by the winning side either. Hundreds of the keenest and most ingenious minds in England and America, with the help of the finest apparatus, were at work trying to undermine the German will to war and with indisputable and enormous victories to provide them with material for propaganda.

In 1944 the Allies, in the face of German boasts, made good their landing in Normandy, broke out of the Cotentin, won a great victory at Falaise, and advanced to the Rhine. This was the moment when the Nazi state might be expected to fall apart, when the rats might be expected to leave the sinking ship, when the discontented might be expected to rise in rebellion. It is hard to discover anything of the sort. There were no major defections at all. The defence of Cherbourg was feeble, but no feebler than might have been expected of an army in the moment of defeat. Isolated German forces continued to defend themselves. No German general declared for the Allied cause; no body of German troops mutinied or offered even passive disobedience to their superiors. On the other hand the German army pulled itself together, backed by a German people who had been subjected to an unceasing rain of bombs as well as to ceaseless propaganda, and the Allied armies were brought to a halt, lasting for months, on the Rhine. The war ended not with the collapse of the German army but with its destruction, while the fighting continued even into the streets of Berlin, into the last ditch.

It is begging the question to point to the iron grip that the

Nazi party maintained over the German people, and to the ferocity and omnipresence of Himmler's police. It was the object of propaganda to loosen that grip, to enfeeble those police by one means or another, and it failed demonstrably and lamentably, and totally. Was there ever the least chance that Joyce would have met with any success with the British public or the British armed forces?

He won for himself the intense hatred of a section of the British public. The bitterest hatred stems from unreasoning fear, and in some minds the quality of Joyce's voice inspired that kind of fear. But at the end of the war there were more people who laughed at him than feared him, and probably more still who were mildly interested in him as a figure in the public eye, and who entertained no strong feelings about him. He had stuck to his post to the end; some of his later broadcasts—probably composed without interference from his paymasters—attained a certain dignity. His fate was closing in upon him from the west and from the east and he knew there was only a miscroscopic chance of his escaping arrest. On April 30th, 1945, he made his last broadcast from Hamburg, with the Allied forces in the very suburbs. It was a reasoned, calm argument, so calm that it made not one single reference to the Jews. The theme was the danger to future peace resulting from the aggrandizement of Russia. Many of the things he said were already in the minds of far-seeing statesmen; within a year or two they would be on their lips. He spoke about 'the growing threat of Soviet Imperialism to British interests; Stalin takes the whole world to be his province', and he is the 'Red dictator whose power today constitutes the greatest threat to peace'. Finally Joyce asked whether Britain could survive. 'I am profoundly convinced that without German help she cannot.'

Those were the very last words he ever spoke into a microphone. His statement after his arrest was almost entirely devoted to the same theme, although a reference to the Jews slipped in. He seemed to be entirely obsessed with the need for

Anglo-German co-operation; and it should be remembered that in a few years England found herself assisting in the re-armament of Germany. He might have been sincere; he might have been wrong-headed enough to believe that co-operation with Hitler would have been Britain's best policy. On the other hand a self-seeking traitor in the same circumstances would have seen clearly enough that the arguments he was putting forward provided the only possible justification—or, at least, the only possible excuse—for his behaviour. It should be remembered against him that he joined forces with Hitler only after the latter's agreement with Stalin, and that when he began to broadcast Nazi armies were joining hands with Red forces in Polish territory. There can be more than one opinion about William Joyce; the reader can take his choice.

He had not had the easiest of lives in Germany; his pay was modest rather than lavish, and he had been treated with notable lack of consideration, not to speak of lack of deference. But when the danger grew imminent his paymasters did their best for him, providing him with false papers which might give him one chance in a thousand of evading capture. He did not exploit that one chance to the uttermost. He wandered miser-ably in the fields and woods for a short time, and then ad-dressed himself to the first British officers he met. He had only to speak to them in English for that famous voice to be in-stantly recognized. They asked him if he were William Joyce, and when he reached for his papers they believed him to be drawing a weapon, and one of them shot him in the leg. It was only a flesh wound, from which he soon recovered, but the wound may have had some influence on his fate. At the moment of his arrest a new Treason Act was under the con-sideration of Parliament, and it was passed one day before he was deemed sufficiently recovered to be flown back to England for trial. Under the new procedure dictated by this Act trials for treason are swifter and less cumbersome, but there are many lawyers of the opinion that justice is not properly safe-guarded. Joyce happened to be the first man to be tried under the new procedure; his trial was absolutely fair, but his life was shortened.

At his preliminary appearance at Bow Street he showed no sign of his wound; he appeared slightly drawn and haggard, but at each subsequent appearance that effect was less and less marked; under sentence of death William Joyce actually put on weight. What everyone noticed who saw him was the odd contrast between his physical appearance and the voice that they knew so well. He was insignificant, dapper, mincing, almost frail, not in the least the burly and blatant creature the voice suggested.

When awaiting trial he had heard of the deaths of his father and his mother; the charming little house in Dulwich where he had spent some years of his youth had been destroyed by a bomb during the early days of the Blitz, but his world had not entirely changed. There was still a devoted younger brother, and there were still a few friends—old members of the British National Socialist League—who stood by him and attended every moment of his trial and of his appeals. It was to them that he waved goodbye, with a gesture that was an odd mixture of gaiety and dignity, when he ran down the steps that lead to the cells from the dock after hearing sentence of death passed on him.

He had been found not guilty on the two counts which had alleged that as a British subject he had given aid to the King's enemies—the evidence which proved he was not a British subject was absolutely conclusive. But he had been found guilty on the third count, that 'being a person owing allegiance' he had contrived to 'aid and comfort the said enemies'. Mr. Justice Tucker had ruled that as a point of law he was such a person as a result of holding a British passport. His two appeals against this ruling were both dismissed. While Joyce's appeal was still under the consideration of the House of Lords Mosley held a public meeting of his followers which Quentin Joyce attended. The newspapers gave the affair a good deal of attention, and the public was greatly disturbed. It may have been this incident which deprived Joyce of his last hope; the Home Secretary refused to grant a reprieve, and Joyce was hanged at Wandsworth Prison, three and a half months after being sentenced, seven months after his arrest. In those seven months the famous voice had uttered only two words in public —'Not guilty'.

ERIC LINKLATER

The
Murder of Darnley

1

THE COURSE OF EVENTS

I HAVE before me, in an illustrated gazetteer of Scotland, a drawing of Craigmillar Castle, which is near Edinburgh. The caption asserts that here, 'in 1566, Mary, Queen of Scots, in company with Bothwell, plotted the murder of Darnley'.

That assertion I say is false; and certainly the charge cannot be proved. It is, however, a charge that has been repeated, and widely believed, for nearly four hundred years, and all who maintain that the Queen was privy to the murder of her husband point complacently to the fact that within three months of his death she was married to the other conspirator—or alleged conspirator—James Hepburn, Earl of Bothwell.

The principals in the case were young. Mary herself was twenty-four, Darnley only twenty-one; Bothwell about ten years older than Darnley. It is easy, then, to find an apparent motive for the murder, and denounce a *crime passionel*. But enquiry into the Queen's character does not support this explanation, and the manner in which Darnley met his death was so extraordinary as to create a mystery that still clamours for solution. It was, indeed, a curiously loud and blatant murder. There was an explosion, in the dark of the night, that woke all Edinburgh, and left, for evidence of murderous intention, two dead bodies lying almost naked on the snow-sheeted soil of a garden. The bodies were unmarked by death, and beside them was a large wooden chair.

But before measuring the chair and its significance the suspects and the important victim will have to be scrutinized, and the events which led to murder must be told. They were not private persons who were involved, and politics cannot be excluded from the story. What had happened, and what might happen because of it, were of interest to Spain and England, as well as to Scotland.

Mary was already acquainted with danger and violence and death. Married before she was sixteen to the Dauphin Francis, a puny boy a year younger than herself, her marriage had made her Queen of France for eighteen months until Francis died, apparently of a mastoid abscess, in the late winter of 1560. In the following summer Mary, a devout Catholic, came home to a Scotland distracted by the zeal of Reformation and dominated by a roughly self-seeking and quite unscrupulous nobility.

The mouthpiece, if not always the leader, of the Reformation was John Knox, who was supported by the so-called Lords of the Congregation: Protestant magnates who had good political and selfish reasons for their acceptance of a chilly doctrine. The Protestant lords were suspicious of Mary and her intentions; Knox addressed her with aggressive and calculated rudeness. Despite these obstacles the first four years of her reign were almost peaceful, and for that interval of grace —rare enough in Scotland—her people had to thank Mary herself, who behaved with prudence, patience, and a judicious firmness; while she was indebted chiefly to her half-brother, the Lord James Stewart, later Earl of Moray, and to Maitland of Lethington, both of whom had close associations with England.

Mary's return, as a young widow, had aggravated the difficulties of her cousin Elizabeth. She, nine years older than Mary and still unmarried, was simultaneously courted by suitors attracted by the wealth of her country, and menaced by the Catholic powers which resented the strength of English Protestantism. Now Mary on the Scottish throne offered a new matrimonial target; she, a grand-daughter of Margaret Tudor, sister of Henry VIII, had a claim to the English throne which in the opinion of many bettered that of Elizabeth, who was illegitimate in the view of Catholic Europe and by decree of Henry VIII and his Parliament. The choice of a husband for Mary—or, rather, the exclusion of politically undesirable husbands—became a matter for anxious thought in London, and it was probably a desire to confuse the issue, or postpone a decision by Mary, that in 1565 induced Elizabeth and her ministers to let a young man called Henry Darnley go north to the other kingdom.

Darnley's father, the Earl of Lennox, had for many years been an exile in England; Darnley was Mary's cousin—like her, a grandchild of Margaret Tudor—and on the other side fetched his descent from the Stuart kings of Scotland. He was a pretty boy, uncommonly tall, whose weak and vicious nature was concealed by an amiable habit, some indoor graces such as a talent for music, and a burlier taste for hunting. Mary met him at Stirling, and in Stirling Castle Darnley had the good fortune to fall ill with measles. Mary nursed him, and in the intimacy of the sick-room—to which she had been accustomed by the recurrent fevers of her miserable little French husband and her own childish ailments, which were many—she fell disastrously in love with him.

News of their attachment alarmed Elizabeth, who had not foreseen so warm a welcome for the returning exile: she herself kept closer guard on her affections. Darnley, through his grand-mother, had also a claim to the English throne, and two good claimants in a wedding bed might become a serious threat to a disputed crown; Elizabeth commanded his return to England, but in vain. In Scotland, where Darnley had quickly made enemies, Mary was resolved to marry him, and married they were, at Holyrood House, on July 29th, 1565. Mary wore black, but danced in the evening, and on the following day Darnley was proclaimed King. None of the nobles present applauded the proclamation save Lennox, his father, who loudly cried, 'God save his Grace!'

Darnley's most determined enemy was Moray, the Queen's half-brother. He, an illegitimate son of James V and leader of the Protestant lords, was an Anglophile and paid by England. He saw the Queen's marriage as a dangerous move in what many believed to be Mary's covert intention to re-establish Catholicism. Darnley was a Catholic, though with no apparent zeal for his Church, and looked like a reinforcement for the Queen's declared intention to retain her personal allegiance to Rome; and a possible ally if she should ever go back on her promise to maintain her subjects' right to worship in accordance with the Protestant rule.

Moray, who had fallen into disfavour before the marriage, led the Protestant lords in a rebellion that gave the Queen the pleasure of a little warlike exercise. Already, in a small northern campaign against the unruly Gordons, she had shown her fondness for riding like a trooper and harrying her enemies through foul weather and rough country; and now she displayed vigour and alacrity—though little judgement or military skill—in pursuit of Moray and his fellow dissidents. She was still popular, and had no difficulty in raising an army. Bothwell was recalled from exile, but not to command it. A couple of years earlier he had been accused of treason by the lunatic Earl of Arran, and Moray, who detested him, had had him imprisoned in Edinburgh Castle from which he had escaped—in darkness, down the rock—and fled to England, then to France. But now that Moray was an outlaw there was room again for Bothwell, who was made Lieutenant of the East, West, and Middle Marches. Command of the royal forces, however, was given to old Lennox, and Moray escaped over the Border to safety in Carlisle; Elizabeth had encouraged and helped to pay for his rebellion, though she had not sent him the three hundred soldiers she had promised.

Wearing a gilt breastplate and morion, Darnley rode with Mary on what was known as the Chase-about Raid—there was no fighting—but when that excitement was over he began to tire, it seems, of his royal responsibilities. Maitland of Lethington, Mary's astute and able Secretary, had also deserted her; he had withdrawn from public affairs until he could be quite sure which side was going to win. It was during this period, when she was without her customary advisers, and Darnley's skill as a lutanist was no substitute for graver abilities, that Mary sought help from another musician, an Italian called Rizzio.

David Rizzio had come to Scotland in the train of one Moretta, an ambassador from Savoy, and first gained the Queen's attention by his ability to sing bass in a quartet of 'varlets of her chamber'. He is said to have composed several airs long remembered and popular in France, and to have been 'a merry fellow', though lacking the advantage of good looks; both friends and enemies agreed that he was black-avised and ill-favoured. Estimates of his age vary from twenty-eight to fifty, and early hardship may have worsened his appearance. But he was clever, he became the Queen's French secretary, and there is no reason for astonishment in the discovery that she preferred his company to that of the surly Calvinists and titled ruffians who filled her court.

Her friendship with Rizzio, and the freedom with which she showed it, were natural enough, but injudicious; and for the first time in her life her behaviour attracted slander. In her years at the French court, where profligacy was not uncommon, and in her first four years in Scotland, where hostile eyes would have been quick to see the earliest prospect of it, there had been no hint or whisper of impropriety in Mary's conduct. The Scots lords, however, resented the sudden promotion of a low-born Italian guitarist, and professed—perhaps illogically— their fear that he was an emissary of the Pope, come to dislodge the precarious structure of Scotch religion. Before his marriage Darnley had been friendly with him, and Rizzio had supported Darnley during the Queen's rash wooing, but this mutual kindness did not endure. Very soon after the marriage there was a rumour, that reached England, of Mary's misconduct with the Italian, and in October Thomas Randolph, a clever and entertaining English agent at the Scottish court, wrote to Cecil, Elizabeth's Secretary of State, to explain the bitter enmity between Mary and her half-brother Moray: she hated him because he knew her guilty secret, he hated her for what she had so basely done. This neat and succinct exposition lacked only truth to commend it.

The breach between Mary and Darnley was now open; he had been persuaded of her infidelity, and was ready to come to terms with his old enemy Moray. In February 1566 Randolph wrote to the Earl of Leicester and told him that Darnley and his father had plans to secure the crown, that Rizzio was to have his throat cut, and Mary's own life might be in danger. At the end of the month he informed Cecil that Lennox was to meet the Earl of Argyll with the promise that if he and Moray would support Darnley's claim to the crown-matrimonial Darnley would bring them home from exile and restore some needed safeguards to the Reformed religion.

The planned assassination, in which other of the Protestant lords were involved, was timed to coincide with the return to Edinburgh of Moray and his fellow exiles, who were to be charged with *lèse-majesté* after the opening of Parliament. It was on March 9th that Rizzio was murdered, at Holyrood House, and this was a crime that left no mystery to tease posterity, but only such incidental questions as whether the fatal blow was struck in the Queen's presence, and if she herself was in danger.

The palace was occupied by troops under the red-bearded, rapacious Earl of Morton and the brutal Lindsay of the Byres. In the Queen's apartments there was a supper-party, small and quiet because it was Lent, and because the Queen was six months pregnant. Rizzio sang for the last time, and Darnley came in and took a vacant chair by the Queen's side. He was followed by the sinister Lord Ruthven, a reputed warlock, who had risen from a sick-bed and wore armour above his nightgown. The other conspirators ran in with naked weapons, and Rizzio clung to the Queen for protection. She herself said his murderers 'struck him over our shoulders with whingers, one part of them standing before our face with bended daggs', but according to another report he was dragged from her presence uttering 'great skirls and cries', and murdered at an outer door.

It was a revolting and atrocious crime, and even after four centuries one may be moved by pity for the wretched Italian minstrel, and detestation of Darnley's cold-blooded treachery. It is, perhaps, unprofitable to meditate on the serviceable mind of Thomas Randolph, who had foreknowledge of the murder, and waited for it, presumably, in calm expectation of the pleasure his masters would derive from the removal of a possible threat to Protestant security; but it is useful to think of, or try to imagine, the feelings of the Queen—not so much of her fear and horror during a few loud and frenzied moments— but rather of her strong stomach and staunch refusal, at the storm-centre of rebellion, to accept defeat. What gave her strength, and dominated her life, was not sensual appetite but a dynastic purpose, and the child in her womb had to be saved to serve that purpose.

Some attempt was made to rescue her when a clamour on the common bell told of outrage, and the Provost with townsmen in armour came hurrying to the palace. Darnley went out to quiet them with an assurance that Mary was safe, but she herself was forbidden to speak to them under pain of being cut 'in collops' and thrown over the wall. Elsewhere at Holyrood were Bothwell and the Catholic Earls of Huntly and Atholl: they, taken by surprise, were powerless to oppose or resist the conspirators, but Bothwell managed to escape.

That night, unattended even by her servants, Mary was alone among her enemies, but she had the wit to recognize a weakness in the confining perimeter, and that weakness was her husband. He came to see her the following morning, and according to Nau (sometime her secretary) she told him, 'You have done me such wrong that neither the recollection of our early friendship, nor all the hope you can give me of the future, can ever make me forget it.' But she appears to have persuaded him to let her ladies attend her, and with the help of Lady Huntly got into communication with Bothwell. In the evening Moray came to condole with her, and protest his innocence. She was glad to see him, and when Darnley returned, to speak for the conspirators and those lately in exile, she was complaisant, realistic, and agreed to overlook all that had happened. She repeated this assurance to Morton, Lindsay, and the abominable Ruthven—who were less easily persuaded of her goodwill than Darnley—and sent for the astute and cautious Lethington. Morton and Ruthven demanded that she sign a document acquitting them of evil act or purpose, and diplomatically she approved it, but postponed her signature. Either Lethington or Darnley was convinced that it was now safe to withdraw the eighty soldiers by whom she was guarded.

To Darnley she spoke gravely and warned him of the danger awaiting him if he kept his friendship with such men as Morton and Ruthven. They, and the other Protestant conspirators, required him to deny his spiritual allegiance to Rome; and how, she asked, would his fellow sovereigns abroad regard his apostasy? She spoke of her own misery, and woke from his shallow mind a transient sympathy. As she later wrote, with studied modesty, to the Archbishop of Glasgow: 'He was induced to condescend to the purpose taken by us, and to retire in our company to Dunbar, which we did under night.'

That gentle statement concealed romantic evasion and a desperate, wild flight. A secret or little-used stairway, a stealthy retreat through kitchens and a cemetery, led to a gate where horses waited, and the Queen mounted behind Arthur Erskine, her esquire of the stables. Her woman, Margaret Carwood, rode pillion behind another, Darnley and an equerry were mounted, a servant brought up the rear. For ten miles they rode hard, to Seton by the coast of the Firth of Forth, and there met soldiers waiting for them. Darnley, in a panic, struck the Queen's horse and called for faster flight. The Queen spoke of the child she carried, and Darnley's comfort was that if he were lost they could make more.

The soldiers were a picket posted by Bothwell. He and

Huntly, and other of their friends, were waiting for the fugitives, and Bothwell declared there was no safety short of Dunbar. They rode on another fifteen miles, and when they arrived, at dawn, the Queen cooked eggs for the soldiers' breakfast. She had the stuff of heroines in her, and the spirit of a great queen; all she lacked was honesty in her subjects and a modicum of loyalty in her advisers.

But Bothwell, though no statesman, had all the courage and peculiar talents of the Border lairds who for more than two hundred years had maintained a precarious power—though from time to time they lost their heads—in the perilous marches between Scotland and England; and now, in the sort of crisis that roused the spirit of all his kind, he raised three or four thousand spearmen from the debatable lands, and Mary, at the head of a sufficient force, returned to Edinburgh, intent not on revenge, but on the pacification of her kingdom.

Some of the rebels submitted at once. Moray swore that he had parted company with the murderers, but wrote to the English Governor of Berwick, commending to his favour his dear friends Morton, Lindsay, and Ruthven. John Knox, with a parting word of praise for those who had justly punished 'that knave David', fled to Ayrshire; and the discreet Lethington retired to the Highlands. Edinburgh welcomed the triumphant Queen, who pardoned more than she punished—Morton and others were outlawed, but two men only were hanged—and publicly accepted Darnley's protestation of innocence. She had seen the two incriminating documents he had signed: that which authorized the murder of Rizzio, the other which declared his intention of taking, with the help of his fellow conspirators, the crown-matrimonial; but to banish Darnley, who was the father of her child and in some sort the King, would have raised a constitutional difficulty as well as the ghost of her brief domestic happiness.

Randolph, the English agent, had been ordered out of Scotland a few days before the murder; an Edinburgh lawyer having confessed that Randolph had given him a subsidy of three thousand crowns for the rebels. Elizabeth declared she had sent them no help at all, and Mary, immediately accepting her cousin's word, offered the soothing explanation that Randolph must have been acting on his own responsibility. Elizabeth, still angry, announced that if Mary would not pardon the Earl of Moray she would find a place for him in England; and Mary, who had already forgiven her half-brother, sent the dulcet reply that she had done so to oblige her cousin.

Something like peace returned to Edinburgh, and what peace there was had been patched up by the Queen's prudence. Her child was born in the castle between ten and eleven in the morning of June 19th, 1566, and in the afternoon Darnley came to see her and his son. She was in a mood of feverish excitement—her labour had been long and difficult—and taunted him a little about his past misbehaviour. One of Bothwell's Border neighbours, who had joined her at Dunbar —John Maxwell, later Lord Herries—recorded their conversation in his *Memoirs*:

'My lord,' she said, 'God has given you and me a son, begotten by none but you!'

The King stooped to kiss the child. She took it in her arms and said again: 'Here I protest to God, and as I shall answer to Him at the great day of judgement, this is your son and no other man's son. And I am desirous that all here, with ladies and others, bear witness; for he is so much your own son that I fear it will be the worse for him hereafter.'

And to another, an Englishman, in that small and over-crowded room: 'This is the son who (I hope) shall first unite the two kingdoms of Scotland and England.'

Volleys of ordnance and popular applause greeted the birth of the child who was to be James the Sixth of Scotland and First of England, and hundreds of bonfires were lighted. Messengers hurried with the news to France and to England, where Elizabeth, dancing after supper, was saddened by the tidings, but recovered her equanimity by the following morning, and presently, for the boy's christening, sent a gold font big enough to bathe him in. Six months later it was melted down and proved even more useful to the mint.

The Queen's peace endured a little while longer, and du Croc, the French ambassador, wrote: 'I never saw Her Majesty so much beloved, esteemed, and honoured; nor so great a harmony amongst all her subjects, as at present is by her wise conduct, for I cannot perceive the smallest difference or division.'

In this precarious harmony the discordant voice was Darnley's. That the Queen retained—obstinately and against all reason—some affection for him is evident in the long and detailed will she made before the birth of her son; among the bequests to Darnley was a diamond ring, enamelled in red, against which she wrote: 'It was with this that I was married; I leave it to the King who gave it to me.' In August there was a brief reconciliation that Darnley spoilt by his now settled hostility to Moray; both Moray and Lethington were again in favour, and such was the general amity that on the last day of September the lords of the Privy Council told the King he should thank God for giving him so wise and virtuous a wife.

There were those, however, who later recalled, or pretended to recall, from this period her increasing friendship with Bothwell and demonstrations of compromising affection. She made a little sea-voyage with him from Newhaven to Alloa, during which, it was observed, she 'joyit to handill the boysterous cabilis'; for the most innocent of pleasures could be darkened by enemies who had no scruples and a purpose to serve. A truly remarkable story—offered, in due course, as evidence of her immorality to her English judges—was invented by the great Latinist, George Buchanan, who, when a professor at Bordeaux, had had Montaigne among his pupils, and was later to be young King James's intolerant tutor. He, with his indisputable genius, found a background for his *conte drolatique* in the Exchequer House in Edinburgh, where Mary lodged for a few days. It was a house with pleasant gardens, and adjoining them was another house in which one of Bothwell's servants lived.

The infant Prince's wet-nurse was Margaret Reres, whom Buchanan changes into a bawd of redoubtable figure: 'very heavy, both by unwieldy age and massy substance'. One night she is said to have conducted Bothwell through the gardens to the Queen's room and left him there to rape her. Not content with that, Mary, some nights later, sent for her bawd and with the help of her woman Margaret Carwood let her down into the garden on a string. The string broke, down fell the massy substance of Margaret Reres, but, undeterred by accident, up she got, ran to Bothwell's chamber, and there dragged him, half naked and half asleep, out of the arms of his wife and conveyed him to the eagerly awaiting Queen.

Till fairly recent times this nonsense was believed by many, even by some who were accepted as historians. That Bothwell stood high in the Queen's favour was true enough; in October she was said to hold him 'in honour above every subject that she hath', and after his good service at Dunbar that was no more than his due. But it was premature to infer the intimacy of rape.

In that month she did indeed nearly kill herself to be with him when he was, as she thought, dangerously wounded. She went to Jedburgh to a justice court, and while there heard that Bothwell, badly hurt in a Border scuffle, lay at the castle of Hermitage, thirty miles away. With Moray and some others she rode there and back in a day, and fell desperately ill on her return. For nine days she was tortured by the barbaric therapy of her doctors, and survived both them and an intestinal haemorrhage; Lethington, with unexpected sympathy, diag-nosed also a broken heart—broken by Darnley's ingratitude. Lethington's opinion may have been not far from the truth, and her sixty miles on horseback was more probably a flight from the bleak reality of her marriage than a love-sick gallop to Bothwell's bed. From this distance in time it looks rather like a boyish escapade, comparable with the pleasure she took in riding with her troopers in the Chase-about Raid, or handling the 'boysterous cabilis' in the little ship sailing to Alloa.

Bothwell recovered quickly from his wounds, but Mary's convalescence was slow and unwilling. She spoke of the misery that Darnley had brought her, she talked of suicide. But by December she had recovered spirit enough to make arrangements for the baptism of her son. The ceremony was conducted, in Stirling, with some magnificence and according to the rites of the Roman Church; though Mary, despite her devotion and the fact that the officiating priest was the Primate of Scotland, refused to let 'a pocky priest spit in her child's mouth'. Darnley, though living in Stirling, was not present at the ceremony.

At Craigmillar Castle, a little while before, there had been serious conversations about the possibility, and advisability, of a royal divorce. Moray and Lethington were, perhaps, the first to think of it; if they offered to procure it Mary might agree to recall Morton and his associates from banishment. Bothwell, Huntly, and Argyll agreed with them. Lethington argued their case with the Queen, who gave her provisional consent subject to the reasonable conditions that the divorce should be legally obtained, and that it would in no way prejudice the status of her son. No immediate steps were taken to ask approval of Parliament, or procure a bill of divorcement, but on Christmas Eve Mary authorized a pardon for Morton and seventy others who were implicated in Rizzio's murder. And early in the new year, in Glasgow, Darnley shelved for ever the prospect of a legal divorce by falling seriously ill.

Some said he had been poisoned; others that his disease was scabies, smallpox, or the other pox. Buchanan, the ingenious Latinist, was responsible for the first suggestion, which may be ignored; and the sufferers from scabies are rarely bed-ridden. The only evidence for a venereal infection was found in a skull that was not conclusively identified as Darnley's, and smallpox may be accepted as the disease from which in fact he was suffering. A rumour circulated, as vague as these several diagnoses, that he had been plotting to crown the infant Prince and declare himself Regent of Scotland. It travelled as far as France, and home again. It kept Mary from hurrying at once to Glasgow—where her natural impulse would have sent her—but on January 20th she wrote to her ambassador in France to tell him of her continuing goodwill to her sick husband, and deplore his constant hostility to her; and that day she set out to bring him back to Edinburgh.

By the end of the month Darnley lay at Kirk o' Field, where on February 10th he was murdered.

2

BLAST

Kirk o' Field, just inside the city wall, was not far from where the Old Buildings of Edinburgh University now stand; perhaps, on a modern map of Edinburgh, near the corner of College Street and Nicholson Street. It had been an ecclesiastical foundation, but since the Reformation the church had fallen into ruin. The old Provost's House, where Darnley lodged, was a solid stone-built structure consisting of a long narrow hall connected by a spiral stairway to the two-storeyed main part of the building, which stood on a steep slope. In the top storey were the King's room, an ante-room, and a gallery that projected on to the city wall. In the lower storey was the Queen's room, and underneath, perhaps extending the whole length of the building, a basement divided into servants' quarters, kitchen, and cellars. The situation was pleasant, and agreeably remote from the bustle of the town; a garden and a little orchard lay beside the house.

Two questions obtrude: the first, why did Mary bring her invalid husband back to Edinburgh? The second, why did she choose to lodge him at Kirk o' Field?

The answer to the first is partly political, partly domestic. There was the rumour—briefly referred to at the end of the previous chapter—that Darnley was involved in a plot to establish himself as Regent of Scotland. This, which may be called the Catholic plot, will be considered in more detail later on; for the moment it is enough to say that the rumour was circumstantial enough to suggest the advisability of keeping Darnley under surveillance. The Queen herself, however, may well have had a simpler motive: she was a woman, and her husband was ill. She had nursed him through measles, she would nurse him through smallpox. (She was immune, she had had the disease herself, and escaped its blemishes by skilful treatment.) Sickness has often bridged loss of affection, and Mary, as well as an obstinate tenderness for her worthless husband, may well have had a woman's native belief that when it came to the management of a sick-room she knew best.

As to the second question, the answer seems to be that it was not Mary who chose Kirk o' Field but Darnley himself. There is evidence that she had intended taking him to Craigmillar, but Darnley preferred Kirk o' Field because—according to Nau, sometime the Queen's secretary—he was sensitive about his appearance, and wanted no one to see him till his pock-marks were healed; he wore a taffeta mask to hide them. While Melville, Mary's envoy to England, said that Darnley was attracted to Kirk o' Field by its remoteness, its gardens, and its healthy situation. He who recommended Kirk o' Field to Darnley may have been Sir James Balfour, a lawyer who, some twenty years before, had rowed in the same ship with John Knox when, after the murder of Cardinal Beton, they were both condemned to the galleys; but since then he had reverted to Catholicism. The house at Kirk o' Field belonged to his brother, who was Canon of Holyrood. The French ambassador, du Croc, was later to name James Balfour as the real traitor in the business.

However that may be, Darnley was installed in the old Provost's House, and two rooms—the upper and lower bedrooms, and also the anteroom—were furnished with sufficient comfort. There was a bed covered with purple for Darnley, and in the room below a small bed, with green and yellow damask and a fur coverlet, for the Queen. She slept there on February 5th and 7th.

On the following Sunday there was a wedding at Holyrood House, where Bastien, a faithful servant, was marrying one of the Queen's women; there was also a semi-official banquet for the ambassador from Savoy. Moretta, in whose train the hapless Rizzio had come, was in Scotland again. The Bishop of Argyll was Moretta's host, and strangely absent from the banquet were Moray, with no better excuse than a pregnant wife; Lethington, with a newly married wife; and Morton, for the substantial reason that he was not yet welcome at court.

From the Bishop's lodging in the Canongate the Queen rode to Kirk o' Field, where she had promised to spend the last night of Darnley's quarantine. His bedroom was uncomfortably crowded, for the Earls of Bothwell, Huntly, Argyll, and Cassilis were playing dice there; the Queen sat in a high chair upholstered in purple to match the bed; and there must have been servants coming in and out. Elsewhere in the house, in the long hall, there were presumably a good many other people, for a Queen and her great nobles do not go unattended.

For perhaps a couple of hours there was conversation of a friendly sort—the Queen's amiability was noted, and afterwards recalled as if amiability were unusual in her—and then she remembered a promise she had made. She had said she would dance at Bastien's wedding-party. She must, she said, return to Holyrood House. Darnley protested, tried to persuade her to stay, but she insisted on keeping her promise. To comfort him, as if he were a fretful child, she gave him a ring before she left. According to Nau, she met, as she was going out, a servant of Bothwell's known as French Paris, and said to him, 'Jesu, Paris, how begrimed you are!' Then, with torches about her, she went back to Holyrood.

Darnley was left with Taylor, his valet, who slept in his room. There were two other servants in the gallery that jutted on to the city wall, and a couple of grooms elsewhere in the building.

About two o'clock in the morning of the 10th an explosion demolished the Provost's House and woke Edinburgh with a roar like thunder. It brought out the magistrates, it brought out frightened people. At Kirk o' Field there was a great heap of rubble, and among the tumbled stones a mutilated body.

The bodies of the King and Taylor, his valet, lay in the garden near a pear tree. There was snow on the ground, and they wore nothing but their night-shirts. Neither body was marked in any way. It was reported that some women who lived nearby had heard the King's voice crying, 'Pity me, kinsmen, for the love of Him who pitied all the world!' The instinctive dramatist is usually at hand when catastrophe occurs.

Official enquiry proceeded slowly, but a story was eventually concocted. It relied on evidence extracted under torture from four men: Dalgleish and Powrie, who were Bothwell's tailor and his porter, and his kinsmen John Hepburn of Bolton and Hay of Talla. The brutal ingenuity of the rack, the pincers, and the boot was never remarkable for its discovery of the truth, and more competent inquisitors might have extracted, from all that torment, a tale that would bear examination.

The report of the Justice Clerk alleged that Bothwell had brought a quantity of gunpowder from Dunbar and deposited it in his quarters at Holyrood House. He had also ordered a powder-barrel. At ten o'clock on the evening of Sunday the 9th, Powrie and another man had orders to take the gun-powder to the Blackfriars Gate, about two hundred yards from Kirk o' Field. It was packed in bags in a leather portmanteau and a trunk; and with a grey horse for transport, two trips were necessary. At the Blackfriars Gate, already opened, were other of the conspirators, and the bags of powder were carried into the garden of the Provost's House. Powrie and his companion took the empty portmanteau and trunk back to Holyrood while the others bore the powder to the back door of the house, which French Paris unlocked. The barrel was too big to go through the door and was left in the garden. The bags were emptied in a heap on the floor of the Queen's room, where Hay of Talla and John Hepburn remained in charge.

French Paris went up to the King's room to tell Bothwell that all was ready; and the Queen and her party left the house. At Holyrood Bothwell changed into workaday clothes, and with Paris returned to Kirk o' Field. (The report goes into detail about his movements, and if it is true it would seem that wherever he went, and whatever he did, he took pains to be recognized). At two o'clock Hay of Talla and John Hepburn lit the fuse and left the house to join Bothwell. The fuse burnt slowly, and Bothwell, impatient, was about to look in through a window, to see what was happening, when the powder blew up. The conspirators ran off, some by one road, some by another. Bothwell returned to Holyrood and called for a drink.

Hepburn and Hay, Powrie and Dalgleish, having served their purpose, were hanged and quartered; and the story they are alleged to have told was believed by many in their own times, and many since. But even within the scope of ordinary criticism —the scope of common sense—it is quite implausible. That Bothwell had stored his gunpowder in Holyrood House seems improbable, for a start. That his servants could load a horse with a trunk and a barrel and lead it—not once, but twice— to Kirk o' Field on that busy Sunday evening, without comment or enquiry, strains credulity. That bags of powder could then be carried into the Queen's bedroom, in a house thronged with people and inquisitive servants, is patently impossible. Nor can one credit the crass and overt stupidity with which Bothwell is said to have identified himself as the arch-plotter—by his insistence on leaving his fingerprints, as it were, on the powder-barrel and the several police posts through which he passed— for Bothwell was an expert and practised adventurer, accustomed to dangerous enterprise and cool evasion. If, indeed, the purpose of the plot had been no more than the elimination of Darnley, is it conceivable that Bothwell, or anyone else, would have wasted time and energy and money on gunpowder when a dagger and discreet bribery could have done the job with a minimum of trouble?

To expose completely the falsity of the official story—of the explanation built by incompetence and dishonesty from the raving of four tortured men—it is necessary to add expert criticism to the criticism of common sense; and it is essential to remember the two facts about the explosion which are attested by all the available evidence. The solid building of the old Provost's House—all its ponderous masonry—was left in a state of total ruin and collapse; and the bodies of Darnley and his valet, on the snowy ground beside the pear tree, were unmarked by violence of any sort.

The first man to consider, with proper care and knowledge, the implications of the total destruction of the house was the late Major-General R. H. Mahon, in his invaluable book *The Tragedy of Kirk o' Field*. Unlike most historians, Mahon knew something about gunpowder, and to begin with he calculated that the maximum amount which a horse could carry, together with a trunk, a portmanteau, and a barrel, in two journeys, was about two hundred and twenty pounds. Now two hundred and twenty pounds of the indifferent gunpowder of the sixteenth century, dumped in a heap in the Queen's bedroom, was most certainly incapable of blowing the Provost's house to smithereens. To produce that effect a cellar beneath the Queen's room must have been packed full of powder, and that could not have been done on a Sunday evening. The cellar was loaded before that animated, that fatal and mysterious Sunday. It may have been loaded before Darnley went to Kirk o' Field, or it may have been loaded while he was there; in which case he was privy to a plot which misfired, and the gunpowder was not meant for him.

The bodies of Darnley and Taylor—here again testimony is unanimous—were unmarked by violence; and the inference, quickly accepted, was that they had not been killed by the explosion but murdered after they had escaped from a threatened house. A noise of some sort, or a smell of smoke, had wakened them, and they had fled to the open ground of the nearby garden, where an allied band of conspirators waited for them. But how, in that cold garden, were they killed? A sword or a cudgel would seem to have been the appropriate weapon, but no deadly cut or lethal bruise was left upon their bodies. Someone suggested that they had been smothered—another thought strangulation by a bow-string probable—but a bow-string would have left its mark, and smothering is a slow business that would not have commended itself to impatient desperadoes waiting for, or lurking under, the terrible eruption that made debris of the Provost's House. Another explanation must be found.

Now the English interest—or perhaps, to be precise, Cecil's interest—in the conflict between Mary and the Protestant lords has been evident from the beginning of the story, and the background of that interest lies in the early history of the Reformation in Scotland, which could not have been achieved without the help of an England intent on establishing a Protestant island in defiance of a Catholic Europe. That Cecil's interest was still lively is attested by an exhibit both informative and fascinating. This is a drawing of the scene at Kirk o' Field, on the morning after the explosion, that was made by an English agent in Edinburgh, and sent by him to London.

The drawing—a composite illustration—shows in its upper right-hand quadrant the corpses of Darnley and Taylor in the garden. Darnley wears nothing but a night-shirt that has been blown up about his chest; Taylor, his buttocks bare, wears a night-shirt equally disarranged, a night-cap, and a slipper on his left foot. Beside them lie a quilt, a dressing-gown, Taylor's belt and dagger, and a wooden chair that seems to be of a substantial kitchen-sort.

Those who offer the explanation that they were alarmed by a scuffle of conspirators or the stink of a burning fuse suggest that Taylor, the devoted valet, picked up Darnley's dressing-gown and the chair to give him some comfort in their flight to the garden; but would even the most devoted of servants, following his master in a hurry down a narrow spiral staircase, have carried a quilt, a velvet dressing-gown edged with sable, and a large kitchen chair? It seems improbable, but that incongruous assortment of undamaged bodies, miscellaneous clothing, and the irrelevant chair demanded explanation, and perhaps no convincing explanation was available until our own experience of things that go bump in the night was enlarged, during the war that began in 1939, by the German Luftwaffe.

In 1940, and the years that followed, many of our cities suffered bombardment from the air, and wherever day dawned upon shattered houses and streets loud with the tinkle of broken glass there were stories of the freakish effects of blast. Londoners in particular learnt the horrors and unpredictability of assault from the air, and most Londoners had their own stories of strange escape and the almost incredible selectivity of a large bomb's explosion. I myself remember a tombstone that entered a half-open window, between heavy curtains, and landed on a bed without doing any damage to the room it had invaded; another great chunk of masonry that flew, again without damage, into a room in Soho and sorely alarmed an elderly lady who found it on her pillow; a girl who was lifted and blown across a room without hurt or visible effect of the blast other than the neat removal of one of her shoes. And there were many stranger tales of escape, by miracle or levitation, from demolished rooms and collapsing houses.

This, surely, is what happened at Kirk o' Field. The cellar loaded with gunpowder blew up like a land-mine, and blew through the shattered roof of the house not only two dead bodies but the quilt, the dressing-gown, and that unnecessary chair. The bodies were, on the surface, unmarked, and there was no pathologist to conduct a post-mortem and establish the cause of death. Darnley's body was, indeed, embalmed; but the embalmers, whoever they were, had little medical knowledge, and a collapsed lung would have told them nothing.

If, then, this explanation is accepted—and no other agrees with the known facts—we are left with three questions, two of which are obviously related, but the third of which may require an extraneous, unconnected answer.

Who loaded the cellar so full? Who were the intended victims? And who lighted the fuse or ignited the powder? These are the questions, and what must be admitted is that he who ignited the powder may have had nothing to do with those who brought it to the cellar. He may have been an opportunist who discovered that the house was mined, and took advantage of an unexpected situation; or the explosion may have been accidental. In the drawing made by Cecil's agent there can be seen the face of a dead man in a heap of rubble, and it is known that a mutilated body was found in the rubble. There were two unnamed grooms in the house, and one of them—drunk on that festive night—may have fallen and let his lantern fall.

But who loaded the cellar? That is the real question, and it will be useful to consider in some detail what has been called the Catholic plot; for a close examination of this, as well as for his knowledge of gunpowder, one is indebted to Mahon.

The plot, if Mahon is right, was drastic and ambitious: its aim the re-establishment of the Roman Church in Scotland, the elimination of the Protestant leaders, and the removal of a Queen whose good sense, and her own dynastic purpose, had not allowed her to lead the Catholic restoration which would have pleased her private faith.

In the background of this reckless project were Pope Pius V and Philip II of Spain. As Fra Michele dell' Inquisizione the Pope had made his name a thing of terror, he was utterly dedicated to the rooting-out of Protestant heresy, and the avowed enemy of England: he hoped to see it overrun by Catholic invasion, and in 1570 he excommunicated Elizabeth. He encouraged Philip in his disastrous attempts to suppress revolt and disaffection in the Netherlands, and Philip was committed to a policy which could not succeed without the defeat of France and England. He had failed to master England by marriage to its gloomy Queen Mary, he was to fail in his attempt to conquer it with his invincible Armada. But he remained stubbornly the champion of his Church.

Against this impressive background the front of the stage is thinly occupied, for in it—looking this way and that for a confidant—stand only Darnley, his father the Earl of Lennox, and the lawyer Sir James Balfour. In May 1566, when Philip of Spain was planning a descent on the Netherlands, Darnley could not keep quiet about his own hope of going there. The Pope's intended legate to Scotland, Vincenzo Laureo, Bishop of Mondovi, was in Paris, and in August he wrote to the Cardinal of Alessandria to say that the difficulties confronting him might be obviated if Philip of Spain should come into Flanders with a strong army; or if 'justice were executed against six rebels whose death would effectually restore peace and obedience' in Scotland. He named them: the Earls of Moray, Argyll, and Morton; Maitland of Lethington; and two lesser men: Bellenden the Justice Clerk, and another official, James MacGill. Laureo thought that Darnley could achieve this 'without any disturbance arising, and with the assured hope that afterwards the holy Catholic and Roman religion could soon be restored'. Magnified by distance, Darnley must have seemed more impressive than his Scottish neighbours had found him; or perhaps the nuncio's faith was stronger than his vision. The only obstacles he could see were the Queen and her uncle, the Cardinal of Lorraine, who out of 'excessive kindness' might refuse their consent.

Mary's uncle, though reluctantly, at last agreed to send a messenger who should encourage her to action on behalf of her Church; and Laureo despatched his own emissaries, the Bishop of Dunblane and the Jesuit Father Edmund Hay. In Scotland Darnley was already talking of the plot: he spoke of it to Mary, who told Moray of the danger he was in. Then Darnley thought of going abroad again, and the Queen heard that he had a ship ready for the voyage. Where he meant to go he refused to say, and left her without ceremony. He wrote complaining letters to the Pope, the King of France, and the King of Spain; he grumbled because three men remained, against his will, in office: Lethington, Bellenden, and MacGill, whom the nuncio had recommended for elimination.

The first messenger arrived in Scotland, and was sadly disappointed by Mary's refusal to have anything to do with his workmanlike proposal to pave the way for a Catholic revival with assassination. She was far from well, and the worst part of her disease, as du Croc believed, was the grief that Darnley caused her. She was desperately intent, about this time, on her plans for the baptism, with due state and dignity, of her infant son; and there were few to help her. To a woman of her faith, and so whole-hearted in her faith as Mary, there may have been temptation to win the favour of a Papal nuncio, and through him of the Pope himself and the greatest monarch in the Catholic world. But she was Queen of her own country, and she had the sagacity, the temperate good sense proper to a queen, as well as the excessive kindness, of which Laureo had complained; and murder was consonant neither with her policy nor her nature.

Laureo's delegates also arrived and found Mary too busy with arrangements for the christening to talk to them. The ceremony was undisturbed, though there were opposing factions in Stirling, and the Protestant lords, now aware of their danger, took steps to reduce Darnley's authority by pledging obedience to the Queen, and not to him, should he and the Queen disagree. It was after this that there were conversations at Craigmillar about the possibility of a royal divorce, and garbled rumours of such discussion—or deliberate distortion—may have bred the story that at Craigmillar a bond was subscribed that committed its signatories to Darnley's murder. What probably occurred was much talk about the menace of the Catholic plot; and Mary was persuaded to give her pardon to the Protestant, powerful, and abominable Earl of Morton.

Now the year turns, and Darnley is brought to Kirk o' Field. In Edinburgh the conspirators had gathered. Moretta, the envoy from Savoy, had returned; and Savoy, a buffer-state between France and Spain, was then pushing out the French and reasserting its friendship with Spain. Moretta had brought David Rizzio to Scotland, and there may have been those who thought it a little curious that now in his company was David's brother Joseph. Father Edmund Hay was there, and the sinister James Balfour, who, if the opinion of two ambassadors is worth anything—du Croc and the Spanish ambassador in London—was certainly implicated in the murder. Old Lennox, at Linlithgow, was not far away, and a ruffian called Ker of Fawdonside—who was said, on fairly good authority, to have threatened the Queen herself when Rizzio was killed—was in the fields beyond the city wall.

But Moray and Lethington were not at Kirk o' Field when the house blew up. After supping with the Bishop of Argyll it was Moretta's job, presumably, to lure them there; and he had failed. Obviously there must have been some arrangement to remove Darnley from the upper room before the fuse was lighted. But everything went wrong—and why? Evidence of the plot is circumstantial, but the evidence of events is that it killed the man whom it was intended to benefit. And how did that happen?

Darnley's loose talk betrayed his fellow plotters and warned the Protestant lords of what was intended. Mary escaped because she remembered her promise to dance at Bastien's wedding-party. Darnley did his utmost to persuade her to stay with him, but she would not. And then, on her way out of the house, she saw French Paris and exclaimed, 'Jesu, Paris, how begrimed you are!' In all the reports of what was said, and what was heard, in that dark winter—evidence extorted from the agony of the rack or a phrase remembered in after years— nothing rings more truly than the innocent surprise of those simple, natural words.

She stayed only a little while at the dance in Holyrood House. Soon after midnight Bothwell and Traquair, the captain of her bodyguard, came to speak with her, and apparently talked long and urgently. Traquair left, and Bothwell argued still. He may have told her that the Catholic plot had been superseded by a counter-plot.

It will be seen later on that a curious connection had been established between Bothwell and Balfour. It will become apparent that in more ways than one the Protestant lords made extraordinary efforts to lay the blame of Darnley's murder on

Bothwell and the Queen. And the conspicuous absence from the Bishop's supper-party of Moray and Lethington, though readily explained by their fear of Catholic violence, may have had a deeper and more immediate meaning.

They may have decided to take advantage of the Catholic plot, and turn it to their own purpose, having nominated other victims. They had every reason to believe that Bothwell and the Queen, as well as Darnley, would be together in the upper room; and there is no difficulty in supposing that their discovery of the plot had made it easy for them to persuade Balfour to change sides and become their agent. The sudden, mysterious, and violent death of Mary and Darnley together would be followed by a morning of panic—the death of Bothwell would remove their most dangerous enemy—and there would be no significant opposition to Moray's assumption of the Regency of Scotland. That this resolution of an intractable difficulty would have pleased Cecil is not open to doubt, though Elizabeth, with genuine anger, would have denounced the crime, and deeply mourned the death of her cousin.

But the counter-plot, if it existed, was no more successful than the Catholic plot of which the embryo never came to full term. Like the garden in the dark scene of Verdi's *Macbeth*, Edinburgh was too full of potential murderers, and the possibility must be admitted that all may have been thwarted by an accident. It is more probable, however, that what thwarted them was the sudden interference of the opportune Bothwell.

Did French Paris, whose begrimed appearance had surprised the Queen, discover the loaded cellar and tell Bothwell what he had found? Or—perhaps and more probably—had he gone down to lock a door or two and make sure that all was ready? If the discovery was made earlier in the day Bothwell had had a few hours in which to persuade himself that here was the chance to realize a latent ambition by removing the prime obstacle to it. But perhaps his mind moved quickly when there was need for haste. This crowded Sunday was Darnley's last night at Kirk o' Field. His period of quarantine would come to an end on the morrow, when the Queen had promised to sleep with him at Holyrood House. And perhaps, by sheer accident, Bothwell found Balfour near the Provost's House before he, Bothwell, set fire to the fuse which had been laid by others.

But before deciding that, the events that followed the explosion must be told.

3

RAPE OF A QUEEN

Some four months after Darnley's death Mary was a prisoner in a small, dank castle on a little island in Loch Leven. She had made the unforgivable mistake of marrying the man who it was widely believed was her husband's murderer. The possibility that fear had driven her to the marriage, which rape precipitated, was ignored by her contemporaries, and has been discounted by historians. It should be useful, however, to see what happened in the weeks that followed the explosion.

According to the rumour which first, and very quickly, reached London and Paris, Darnley's father, the Earl of Lennox, had also been killed; and the Venetian ambassador in Paris wrote that the double murder was 'the work of heretics' —Protestants, that is—'who designed the same for the Queen, intending to bring up the Prince in their religion'. He who sent the news must have been a Catholic agent who, standing ready to report immediately on the effect of the explosion, had had to admit the failure of the plot, and offered as an explanation the intervention of Protestant counter-plotters. He reported the death of Lennox because, having heard that two bodies had been found, he guessed the identity of the other, knowing that Lennox had been expected in Edinburgh to share his son's triumph.

On the very day of the murder Mary, in a letter to the Archbishop of Glasgow, declared her belief that the explosion had been intended for her destruction as well as her husband's; and the following day she received, from the Archbishop, a warning to take heed to herself because of an enterprise 'to be trafficked to [her] contrary'.

On February 12th a minute of the Privy Council records that Mary, with the approval of her Council, offered free pardon and a reward of two thousand pounds to the first who should name the plotters or the murderers; and within a week a bill on the door of the Tolbooth charged Bothwell, James Balfour, and others with the crime, and alleged the Queen's assent. At night, in the dark streets, voices cried that Bothwell had murdered the King. At St. Giles, the Market Cross, the Abbey Gate of Holyrood, and the ports of the city bills were posted to denounce him; and portraits under the superscription 'Here is the Murderer of the King' were scattered through the town. Bastien, the loyal servant, and Joseph Rizzio, brother of David, were also accused.

That these were the citizens' spontaneous denunciations can hardly be credited, and as Lennox was not in Edinburgh—he came as far as Linlithgow, and returned to Glasgow—it seems unlikely that he was responsible for them. That the bills were distributed and the voices hired by Moray and Lethington is the manifest inference; but Mahon suggests, and discovers some curious evidence in support of his theory, that the bills which associated Mary with the murder were the work of English agents.

Bothwell's answer to the charges made against him was a rough defiance. His hand on his dagger, he walked in Edinburgh with fifty Borderers behind him. If he knew who had posted the accusing bills he would wash his hands in their blood, he said. He stood high in the Queen's favour, and is said, for a little while, to have dominated her court. A story that he and Mary played golf together may also be true.

Lennox demanded enquiry into the crime, and asked for the arrest of all whom the anonymous placards accused. The Protestant lords were now making common cause with Lennox and his Catholic friends, and from England Cecil sent his commands for 'the maintenance of God's honour and the punishment of the late murder'. On March 23rd Mary withdrew the objections she had previously made to Lennox's demands—on the ground that the accusations were confused and contradictory—and promised that Bothwell and seven others should stand their trial. Five days later Bothwell reinforced the promise by sitting as a member of the Privy Council that made arrangements for the trial 'according to the laws of the realm'. By this time rumour was already busy with a story that Bothwell was about to obtain a divorce from his wife, Jean Gordon—sister of the Earl of Huntly—and use his freedom to marry the Queen.

Lennox was summoned to appear at the Tolbooth as prosecutor in the trial, and while Bothwell filled Edinburgh with his supporters—to the number of four thousand, it was said—Lennox raised almost as many and marched to Linlithgow. There he was stopped and told to appear at the Court of Justice with only the number of attendants that the law permitted, which was six. He retired to Stirling, and, complaining of illness, asked for a postponement of the action to give him more time to prepare his case.

On April 12th, with Morton and Lethington on either side of him—Moray had discreetly retired to France—Bothwell rode from Holyrood to the Tolbooth, attended by the great train of his supporters, and faced the Lord Justice, Argyll, and a jury that included many of his avowed enemies. The indictment was read—he was accused of 'art and part of the cruel, odious, treasonable, and abominable slaughter of the late, the right excellent, right high and mighty prince, the King's Grace, dearest spouse for the time to our sovereign lady the Queen's Majesty'—and the court sat for seven hours. But no one was there to swear the truth of the indictment or support its charges, and after long debate the Earl of Caithness, foreman of the jury, announced a unanimous verdict acquitting the accused. Without evidence on which to convict, the jury could do nothing else; and Bothwell underlined the verdict by offering to defend his innocence in single combat.

A few days later, when the Queen rode to her Parliament, Bothwell carried the sceptre, and on the nineteenth, when the

Parliament closed, he carried the sword of honour back to Holyrood. That evening he invited twenty-eight peers, prelates, and other notables to supper at the palace, and produced a document which he invited them to sign. The first part recorded his verdict of not guilty, and those present were asked to pledge themselves to take his part in a continuing quarrel; the second part noted the Queen's solitary state, her manifest need of a husband, the good qualities of the Earl of Bothwell—and those present were asked to further the marriage he proposed by their vote, counsel, and assistance. This insolent suggestion was approved, and the extraordinary document received the signatures of eight bishops, nine earls, and seven barons; whether drunk or sober, no one knows.

The Queen had gone to Seton, and there Bothwell followed her; with him went Lethington and Bellenden. Fortified by the promised help of eight bishops and sixteen peers of the realm, he declared his suit. 'He began afar off to discover his intentions unto us and to essay if he might by humble suit purchase our goodwill,' so Mary wrote to the Bishop of Dunblane. He had, in preceding weeks, shown his 'readiness to fulfil all our commandments', and desire 'to entertain our favour by his good outward behaviour'. But the Queen's response was firm and discouraging. Not even the support of eight bishops and sixteen noblemen moved her. She had friends and he had enemies, and neither side, she thought, would permit a marriage for which she herself had no liking. Her final answer was 'nothing correspondent to his desire'.

The following day Mary rode to Stirling to see the infant Prince, now ten months old. With her went Huntly, Lethington, Melville—her sometime envoy to England—and thirty horsemen. She spent a day with the child; on the 23rd slept at Linlithgow. There was a rumour, which Cecil heard, that Bothwell arrived there at midnight, had some talk with his brother-in-law Huntly, and made a proposal which Huntly violently rejected. Bothwell lay at the strong House of Calder, some ten miles away, with eight hundred troopers ostensibly mobilized to deal with thieves in Liddesdale. They were used, instead, to capture a Queen.

Somewhere on the road between Edinburgh and Linlithgow —perhaps where the Gogar burn runs into the river Almond— Mary and her small escort were halted by Bothwell and his troopers. He accosted her politely, and said he had come to save her from a grave danger and take her to the safety of Dunbar; Parliament had lately ratified his appointment as Captain of Dunbar Castle in acknowledgement of his 'great and manifold good service' to Scotland. Some of Mary's company were apparently willing to defend her, but that she would not allow, saying she was ready to go with Bothwell rather than provoke bloodshed and death.

At Dunbar, where they arrived about midnight, Bothwell sought pardon for 'the boldness he had taken to convey us to one of our own houses, whereunto he was driven by force, as well as constrained by love'. His wooing was eloquent and brisk, and to his request that 'it would please us to do him that honour to take him to husband'—Mary is writing to the Bishop of Dunblane—he 'joined thereto all the honest language that could be used in such a case'. Elsewhere in the castle there was more violent argument, for after a quarrel of uncertain origin Huntly tried to kill Lethington, whom Mary herself had to rescue with a fierce display of temper.

When Bothwell's honest language failed to achieve his purpose it seems that he brought his rape or abduction on the Edinburgh road to a logical conclusion by rape in its more specific sense. Melville, who was at Dunbar, says: 'The Queen could not but marry him, seeing that he had ravished her and lain with her against her will.' Others found an explanation of her submission in witchcraft, which Bothwell was thought to practise. Mary herself, in her pathetic letter to the Bishop, wrote: 'We saw no esperance to be rid of him, never man in Scotland once making an attempt to procure our deliverance.' And later in that letter: 'As by a bravado in the beginning he had won the first point, so ceased he never till by persuasions and importunate suit, accompanied not the less with force, he had finally driven us to end the work begun at such time and in such form as he thought might best serve his turn.'

A few days later Bothwell's wife began her suit for divorce, accusing him of adultery with her sewing-maid Bessie Crawford, and on May 3rd four Protestant commissioners gave her the freedom she asked for. Proceedings before the Catholic Consistory were equally satisfactory. That court had been restored in order to deal with the dissolution of Mary's marriage to Darnley, if dissolution should be found advisable, and its authority was now used to declare Bothwell's marriage to Jean Gordon null from the beginning, because no dispensation had been sought to permit marriage within the prohibited degrees; though John Hamilton, the Archbishop of St. Andrews, had given such a dispensation a little more than a year before.

The Queen sought advice from several Catholic bishops, who apparently reassured her. A Privy Council of a sort was held, and the presence of Lethington, the Secretary, may have given it substance. After ten days at Dunbar Mary returned to Edinburgh, at first to the castle—Bothwell, dismounted, led her horse—and then to Holyrood House. Their plans were checked by John Craig, the bold and honest minister of St. Giles, who refused to read the banns and preached against a marriage that was 'odious and slanderous to the world'. But by May 14th the marriage contract was ready, and Bothwell had been made Duke of Orkney and Lord of Shetland; the marriage was celebrated according to the Protestant form, and Mary again wore mourning. There were no public festivities, and there is no evidence that marriage brought happiness to either party.

Lethington wrote: 'From her wedding day she was ever in tears and lamentations, for he would not let her look at anybody, or anybody look at her, though he knew that she liked her pleasure and pastime, as well as anybody'. Melville heard her ask for a knife to stab herself, and du Croc, surprised by the change in her demeanour, was told, 'If you see me melancholy it is because I do not choose to be cheerful; because I never will be so, and wish for nothing but death.' Gossip declared that Bothwell sought comfort from his divorced wife Jean, with whom he spent several days a week.

For a short while, however, the Queen's consort conducted the affairs of state with apparent sobriety and good sense. The Privy Council met, and he wrote diplomatic letters to Elizabeth and her Secretary, and to the Scottish ambassador in Paris. But there was no substance in his pretence to rule, and an attempt to mobilize a great force for action on the Border met no response but preparation for resistance; and Lethington showed which way the wind was blowing by leaving the court without other ceremony than a letter to Cecil asking for financial aid to further rebellion.

On June 6th Bothwell and the Queen, with soldiers and some artillery, went to Borthwick Castle when a force of rebel cavalry, under Morton and Lord Home, was already on the way to the capital. Borthwick was a place of great strength, and easily withstood a brief assault. But Bothwell could not rule Scotland from a besieged castle, and leaving Mary with a sufficient garrison to defend it, he escaped in disguise. The investing cavalry, waiting for the main insurgent force under Mar and Lindsay, grew uneasy and withdrew; and Mary, sending a message to Bothwell, also slipped out in disguise and joined her husband. They rode to Dunbar, and issued a summons calling loyal subjects to their aid.

The insurgents, in the meanwhile, had entered Edinburgh, where Bothwell's final defeat was hastened by a curious decision that he had lately taken. He had removed a loyal and trustworthy officer from command of the castle, and replaced him with James Balfour. It is hardly conceivable that he did this willingly. It is difficult to believe that anyone, of his own volition, would at this date have given Balfour the smallest position of trust; and the only possible reason for Bothwell's disastrous error is that he was blackmailed. Balfour had threatened him with exposure, and demanded command of the castle as the price of his silence. But what sort of exposure could Balfour have threatened that warranted so huge and ruinous a payment? Something that happened on the night of Darnley's murder seems the only possible answer, and what was worth Edinburgh Castle except Balfour's knowledge that Bothwell had fired the fuse? Balfour may have seen him do it.

That he had no sense of loyalty, no conception of fidelity, is made pretty evident by the fact that after a little argument he surrendered the castle to Lethington. Bothwell lost control of the capital, and when he and Mary, with what strength they had been able to muster, advanced to give battle at Carberry Hill, near Musselburgh, there was no fighting but only bluster and half-hearted challenges to single combat. Bothwell's un-disciplined army melted away, the French ambassador became a well-intentioned but unsuccessful mediator, and in the evening Bothwell, with the consent of a Queen who hated bloodshed and the agreement of a rebel army that had no wish to fight, mounted and rode away, unpursued. But the Queen was led prisoner into Edinburgh, where a frenzied mob greeted her with villainous objurgation and fierce cries of 'Burn her! Burn the whore!'

No one can map the huge extent of her distress nor plumb the depths of her misery. Betrayed by one faction after another of her nobles—betrayed again and again by all on whom she had thought to rely—she was now confronted with the hatred of a people for whom she had compromised her faith and won, by her sagacity, a little while of peace in the internecine war of rival dogmas. Total defeat and abject humiliation met her in the stinking streets of her capital; but, though she wept and could not contain her sorrow, she was not yet beaten.

They took her to the island castle on Loch Leven, they demanded her abdication, and she yielded to their demands. She was pregnant by Bothwell's unmannerly assault upon her royalty, and presently miscarried of twins. But this added humiliation, and physical weakness, did not prevent, as the months went by, a resurgence of her spirit and ambition. She escaped, and marvellously gathered a little force again, and vainly offered battle.

That was in May 1568, at the village of Langside, a little way south of Glasgow. She had no hope of success, her ragged army was broken, and Mary fled south to the Solway and crossed its swift tide to the safety and shame of surrender to England. For nineteen years, until her death, she lived in the sanctuary of political imprisonment.

Bothwell, declared outlaw and rebel, tried without success to fight on, tried to gather a fleet, and went north to his nominal dukedom of Orkney. Fortune had deserted him, and he fled eastwards to Norway, where disaster finally caught up with him and clapped him into a Danish prison.

But Moray, now Regent of Scotland, and the Protestant lords had not yet concluded their dispute with Mary. In May or June 1568 Moray sent a man called John Wood to England with Scots translations of certain letters which, if genuine, contained proof of Mary's complicity in murder; and Wood was instructed to ask 'if the French originals are found to tally with the Scots translations, will that be reckoned good evidence?'

The matter of these Casket Letters, as they were to be called, will be considered later. Here it is enough to say that arrangements were presently made for a conference at York that was to be something in the nature of a public trial: of Mary's subjects for rebellion, of Mary herself on darker charges. In October commissioners representing Elizabeth, the imprisoned Mary, and the infant James VI met in York, and presently removed to Westminster. Their findings were inconclusive.

4

CHARACTER OF THE ACCUSED

Swinburne, in a famous article in the eleventh edition of the *Encyclopaedia Britannica*, declared: 'Passion alone could shake the double fortress of [the Queen's] impregnable heart and ever active brain.' Elsewhere he wrote: 'But surely you were something better than innocent!' And soon after her return from France Knox had said of her, 'We call her not a hoor, but she was brought up in the company of the wildest hoormongers, yea, of such as no more regarded incest than honest men regard the company of their lawful wives.'

Alike to moralists and romantics the temptation has been irresistible to portray Mary as a tragic wanton, doomed to shame and persuaded to murder by the passion of her uncontrollable sensuality; and as in the popular explanation of the explosion at Kirk o' Field, there is no evidence whatever to substantiate common opinion.

In her early years in France, and during her first four years in Scotland—this has been noted already—there is no suggestion, or shadow of a suggestion, of any impropriety in her conduct. She was only twenty-five when she became a prisoner in England, and for nineteen years she lived, in open imprisonment and many different places, without slander or suspicion of misbehaviour except on one occasion when, under the guardianship of the Earl of Shrewsbury, his wife—the notorious Bess of Hardwick—was moved by jealousy to propagate a slander; which, on being charged with it, she promptly retracted. Now Mary, when she crossed the Solway, was a very attractive young woman, and in the sixteenth century England had no lack of reckless and virile young men. If Mary had been the honey-pot of romantic legend she might have attracted a dozen lovers, but there is neither record nor whisper of even one.

In Scotland she was twice married, and both her marriages were manifest and immediate, or almost immediate, failures. Let it be admitted that Darnley was a silly, shallow, and vicious young man; but Mary was older than he, she had wooed him with an impetuous, girlish fervour—loading him with gifts, designing his clothes and the decoration of his rooms—and if her enthusiasm for marriage had been matched by any practical ability, or even complaisance, in the marriage-bed, she could surely have kept him faithful, and maintained his loyalty, for a few winter months. But that she failed to do. He quickly tired of her, and turned for amusement to shooting and hunting, or the cultivation of more adaptable young women.

She married Bothwell, and Bothwell was a man who enjoyed the favours of women, and had had considerable experience of women's favour. When he married the Queen of Scots—whether by force or persuasion—his common sense, and appreciation of the position she gave him, must have made him eager to secure a sound connubial alliance by exercise of the gifts which he had practised elsewhere. But Mary, after marriage, openly wept and complained, and threatened suicide.

The inference is—and it cannot be denied—that she had neither aptitude nor liking for the familiarities of marriage. If her girlish affection for Darnley had been substantiated by a normal sexual appetite she could have kept him harmless and faithful; if her dynastic ambition, her political acumen, could have summoned a bedtime amiability to her help she could have shown at least a diplomatic satisfaction in her enforced, but potentially useful, marriage to the hardy Duke of Orkney. But she failed him, as she had failed Darnley; and failed her own cause.

One of the enduring legends of the Queen's reign is the devotion of her four Marys; and without suggesting any perversity of affection, there may be more truth in this than in many of the stories told about her. She had the bold and lively tastes that provoke hero-worship; she had a recurrent enthusiasm for adventure that ignored her physical frailty, and would certainly have roused—if such had been her environment—the enthusiastic devotion of a girls' school. She had enjoyed riding roughly through the harsh Buchan landscape in pursuit of rebellious Gordons, the Chase-about Raid after Moray, and handling sheets and halliards in a stormy little voyage to Alloa. Hero-worship was her due, because she was indeed an heroic creature who complicated assessment of her character by also possessing in abundance the gentlest feminine gifts and aptitudes. She loved little dogs and such dependent creatures as her shiftless husband, but her faculty of love was not of the sort that finds satisfaction in physical abandonment.

A witness to her character—not attached to her by any sympathy with the Scottish cause—is Sir Francis Knollys, who met her in Carlisle when she fled from Scotland, and wrote to Cecil: 'This lady and princess is a notable woman. She seemeth to regard no ceremonious honour beside the acknowledgement of her estate regal. She showeth a disposition to speak much, to be bold, to be pleasant, and to be very familiar. She showeth a great desire to be avenged of her enemies; she showeth a readiness to expose herself to all perils in hope of victory; she delighteth much to hear of hardiness and valiancy, commending by name all approved hardy men of her country, although they be her enemies; and she commendeth no cowardness even in her friends. The thing that most she thirsteth after is victory, and it seemeth to be indifferent to her to have her enemies diminish, either by the sword of her friends, or by the liberal promises and rewards of her purse, or by division and quarrels raised among themselves; so that for victory's sake pain and perils seemeth pleasant unto her, and in respect of victory, wealth and all things seemeth to her contemptuous and vile.'

Of Bothwell many harsh judgements have been recorded. A murderer, brutal and debauched; that turbulent and licentious

Earl; uncouth, unlettered, a man who cared nothing for another's life or a woman's honour—opinions such as these
built for him a common epitaph of infamy, and no one in his
senses would try to erase it for the encomium proper to a man
of saintly character and stainless reputation. But in 1937 a
reassessment of him—of the man and his deeds—was offered
in a balanced, scholarly, and most persuasive biography by
Robert Gore-Browne. This was no attempt to whitewash
Bothwell but it was an attempt—and in my opinion, though I
do not agree with all that Gore-Browne has to say, a successful
attempt—to clear his name of the charges laid by vulgar and
intemperate abuse. At a time when the brutality of casual
manslaughter was a commonplace, it appears that Bothwell
was curiously averse to taking life without good reason, and—
perhaps of greater historical interest—Gore-Browne asserts,
with evidence for his assertion, that Bothwell was singularly
honest.

It was, notoriously, an age when bribery was recognized as
a tidy and convenient instrument of national policy. In 1564 the
Spanish ambassador, de Silva, could report that eight thousand
crowns 'bought Queen Elizabeth the goodwill and secret information of the leading men in Scotland'; Moray got a
salary of five hundred pounds. But Bothwell, though always
poor and plagued by poverty, seems not to have taken bribes.
His Border ancestry was distinguished, and his abduction of
Mary may almost be excused as a family failing, for his unruly
forefathers had not hesitated to woo a queen when a queen
moved their interest; he may have suffered from pride. Nor
was he uncouth and illiterate, but rather a *beau sabreur*, an
adventurer who moved with ease in the lordly circles of France
and England and northern Europe. From his own country he
had inherited a traditional gallantry, and his native authority
commanded the loyalty of his own people.

I do not intend to follow in detail Gore-Brown's careful and
well-documented account of Bothwell's life, though it is of
great value in trying to elucidate the murky—the deliberately

darkened—course of events in Scotland between the years 1561 and 1567. I accept, on the whole, his assessment of Bothwell's character, and I welcome in particular his explication of a 'romantic' episode that conceivably goes some way towards a solution of the irritating problem of the Casket Letters.

Bothwell, as hereditary Lord High Admiral of Scotland, had gone to Copenhagen in 1560, during the Regency of Mary of Lorraine; and there he met Anna Throndsen, daughter of a retired Norwegian admiral, who fell in love with him. She went with him to Flanders, he took her to Scotland. She appears to have lived in a semi-settled state, to have acquired some property, and may have borne him a child. She went back to Norway in 1563 when Bothwell, in temporary disgrace, was in an English prison; but her passport entitled her to visit Scotland as often as she wished. There is no proof that she came again, but Gore-Brown suggests that she returned in 1565, and finds substance for the suggestion in the contents of the casket that held the notorious letters.

As well as letters there was a set of so-called sonnets in a French that Ronsard and Brantôme both agreed was too unpolished, too clumsy, to be Mary's writing; and Gore-Brown's ingenious inference is that they, and at least one of the letters, were written by Anna. Not only the style but what is said in them suits the Norwegian girl and her circumstances better than the Queen and hers: there is a line, for example, that reads: '*pour lui tous mes parents j'ai quitté et amis*'.

By 1567 Anna was back in Norway, in or near Bergen; and when Bothwell fled there, friendless and defeated, from his unrewarding Dukedom of Orkney, his discomfiture was aggravated by Anna's reappearance with a charge of seduction and a claim for return of the money she had lent him, seven years before, to pay for their journey to Flanders.

5

THE CASKET LETTERS

According to a declaration made by the Earl of Morton, he and Lethington were dining in Edinburgh on June 19th, 1567, when 'a certane man came to me, and in secrete maner schew me that thre servants of the Erl Bothwilles wer cumit to the toun, and passit within the castell'. On a sudden impulse, says Morton, he sent out some sixteen of his friends and servants to look for Bothwell's people, and presently an informer offered 'for a meane pece of money' to reveal where they could find one of them, George Dalgleish. The said George was apprehended and threatened with torture at the Tolbooth; whereupon he led his captors to his lodging in the Potterow, and from under a bed produced a locked silver box which, he said, he had removed from the castle on the previous day. The castle, it will be remembered, was commanded by Sir James Balfour; but whether he knew of the casket's existence, or Dalgleish's removal of it, is not recorded.

On June 21st, says Morton, the contents of the casket were inspected by several nobles and gentlemen. Within it, as well as some disputed documents, were nine letters in French, alleged to have been written by Mary to Bothwell, and the French 'sonnets'. Morton, on oath, declared that he had tampered with none of the papers, but Morton's oath need not be taken seriously. Moray, who is usually thought to have been more careful if not more scrupulous than Morton, is known to have perjured himself in the matter, and there are so many contradictions in the charges made against Mary that it is difficult to resist a feeling that all her accusers were trying to invent a plausible tale rather than clarify dispute and disclose the truth.

Patient explication of the whole tortuous argument—of rumour, report, of what was said to have been seen though no one knows who saw it, and of what was alleged to have been signed though no signature remained—may be found in the works of Andrew Lang and T. F. Henderson. And Lang, with an audible sigh, writes: 'The letters are not known to have been seen by any man—they or the silver casket—after the death of the Earl of Gowrie'; who died in 1600.

There is, then, some doubt as to what exactly was studied by the commissioners who assembled in York and removed to Westminster in the autumn and winter of 1578. But there are extant Scots, English, and Latin translations, French translations from the Latin, and—of some of the letters—French versions. Controversy has always lingered most warmly about Letters I and II.[1]

Letter I, written 'from Glasco this Saturday morning'—that is, according to the prosecution, January 25th, when Mary had gone to Glasgow to fetch Darnley, recovering from smallpox, to Edinburgh—begins with Mary's complaint that Bothwell has not written to her, and goes on to say: 'I bring the man Monday to Cregmillar, where he shall be upon Wednesday.... He is the meryest that ever you sawe, and doth remember unto me all that he can, to make me believe that he loveth me. To conclude, you wold say that he maketh love to me, wherein I take so much pleasure, that I have never com in there, but the payne of my syde doth take me. I have it sore today.'

The letter does indeed suggest conspiracy, even though Craigmillar was not, on that occasion, Darnley's destination. But its wicked significance depends entirely on the veracity of two words in the concluding line, 'from Glasco', and anyone could have added these. Gore-Browne suggests that the letter was written not in January from Glasgow but before the christening of the infant James in December, when Mary was vainly trying to persuade Darnley to come to the ceremony. In which case no malignancy can be read into it.

1. The English translations at the Record Office are quoted.

Letter II is a much stranger document. It is, in the first place, of great length: about five thousand words, or nearly a third of the length of this article. It is supposed to have been written from Glasgow, during the four or five days she spent there, and the writing of so long a letter during so short a visit may to some seem a little improbable. To begin with, Mary describes her arrival, and then her conversation with Darnley: 'He told me his grefe, and that he wold make no testament, but leave all unto me and that I was cause of his sickness for the sorrow he had, that I was so strange unto him. "And [said he] you asked what I ment in my letter to speak of cruelty. It was of your cruelty who will not accept my offres and repentance I avow that I have done amisse, but not that I have also always disavoued; and so many many othir of your subjects don and you have well pardoned them. I am young. You will say that you have also pardoned me in my time and that I returne to my fault. May not a man of my age for want of counsel faylle twise or thrise and mysse of promis and at the last repent and rebuke himself by his experience?" '

He excuses himself more pitifully: ' "And when I offend you sometimes, you are cause thereof: for if I thought, when anybody doth any wrong to me, that I might for my resource make my moan thereof unto you, I wold open it to no other, but when I heare anything being not familiar with you, I must keep it in my mynd and that troublith my wit for anger." '

He is unhappy about his appearance—'he hath no desyre to be seen'—and this careful record of so much self-pity contrasts very oddly with the description in Letter I of a man who 'is the meryest that ever you saw'. It is impossible to believe that Mary, writing twice within four or five days, could have written such contradictions; if II is thought credible, then I was *not* written 'from Glasco this Saturday morning'.

In Letter II Mary tells Darnley that she is going to take him to Craigmillar, and he pleads with her not to leave him. She writes: 'If I had not proof of his hart to be as waxe, and that myne were not as a dyamant, no stroke but comming from your hand wold make me but to have pitee of him.' And how uncomfortable one feels when reading that! For such rhetoric is not in tune with Mary's voice.

The letter becomes disjointed. A paragraph begins, without relevance to the preceding paragraph: 'I think they have bene at school togither. He has allwais the tears in his eye. He saluteth every man, even to the meanest, and maketh much of them, that they may take pitie of him.' Then she writes that she hates the necessity of dissembling; and a few lines later: 'Excuse me if I write ill.' But that's the apology of some meek little, modest little, damp little nobody, and more ludicrously unlike the Queen's voice than the noisy rhetoric about diamond hearts!

'I am weary,' she writes, 'and am asleepe, and yet I cannot forbear scribbling so long as there is any paper. Cursed be this pocky fellow that troublith me thus much, for I had a pleasanter matter to discourse unto you but for him. He is not much the worse, but he is yll arrayd. I thought I shuld have been kylled with his breth, for it is worse than your uncle's breth; and yet I was sett no nearer to him than in a chayr by his bolster, and he lyeth at the further syde of the bed.'

In a later paragraph there is this: 'I have not seen him this night for ending your bracelet, but I can fynd no clasps for yt. . . . Send me word whether you will have it and more monney, and how farr I may speak.'

And Letter II comes to an end in this way: 'Excuse my evill wryting, and read it over twise. . . . Pray remember your friend, and wryte unto her and often. Love me allwais as I shall love you.'

In these three passages I suggest that 'cursed be this pocky fellow' is an interpolation, put in for an obvious purpose; that as Mary was returning to Edinburgh within a day or two it would have been absurd for her to tell Bothwell to write to her and she would send him some money; that a second apology for her handwriting is again out of character; and that the Queen of Scots was unlikely to plead, with suburban coyness, 'Pray remember your friend.'

Letter II has some admirable passages, and perhaps Mary wrote parts of it—several parts—though this one cannot say for certain because one does not know how many women in Scotland would write well, who were or had been separated from their lovers, and whose letters might have been stolen. But it takes a long time to write five thousand words in an Italian hand, and I cannot believe that Letter II was written at a sitting, nor can I see the necessity of writing so much to a man who would hardly have time to read it before the supposed writer was with him. There are, moreover, phrases in it that echo other situations, and phrases that smell of coarser hands.

What, then, is finally to be said?

Where liars abound, and all the evidence is nearly four hundred years old, the seeker for truth is like a benighted traveller feeling for a path of safety through a land of treacherous bogs and marshes, impelled only by a conviction that a solid road exists which may be found by the careful tapping of his stick.

In my search for truth, solid ground—as I think—has been discovered by the circumstantial evidence, which I say is conclusive, of Mary's character; by Major-General Mahon's detection of the absurdity of the official story that was put out to explain the destruction of the house at Kirk o' Field; by the evidence, that London made available after 1940, of the incalculable effects of high explosives, and the consequent exposure of the true cause of Darnley's death; and by the frenzied and clearly dishonest testimony concocted by Moray and Lethington in the Casket Letters to inculpate Mary and exculpate themselves.

And so, with some confidence, I bring this short study to its conclusion with an explanation of what led to the explosion at Kirk o' Field; of what happened there; and of what happended thereafter. And because so much in the story has been qualified by 'perhaps' or 'it seems', 'it is probable' or 'according to'—a repetition that grows very tiresome—I shall tabulate my findings and offer them as statements of fact.

1. There was a Catholic plot, devised with the approval of Pope Pius V and King Philip II of Spain, to remove Mary from the throne of Scotland because she, a good Catholic, had failed in her Catholic duty to restore in Scotland the authority of Rome. The Scottish principals nominated for prosecution of the plot were Darnley, his father the Earl of Lennox, and Sir James Balfour. Among the agents or official observers were Moretta, the Bishop of Dunblane, and Father Edmund Hay.

2. Through Darnley's indiscretion the Catholic plot was discovered by the Protestant lords. They, with the knowledge and connivance of Queen Elizabeth's Secretary Cecil, found means of subverting the Catholic plot to their own advantage, and to the advantage of an England determined to maintain a Protestant bastion against the constant offensive of Catholic Europe. Queen Elizabeth herself remained in ignorance of this connivance.

3. James Balfour, widely suspected as the arch-villain, had easy means of loading the cellar with powder because his brother owned the house in the precincts of Kirk o' Field. Discovery of the Catholic plot let the Protestant lords coerce him, by menace or bribery, into an exposure of the means intended and prepared for assassination of the Queen. They decided to use the powder that he had bought to blow up Mary, Darnley, Bothwell, and such of their friends as might be with them.

4. At some time on Sunday, February 9th, Bothwell discovered that the house was prepared for explosion. After Mary's return to Holyrood House, Bothwell and Traquair told her that there was a plot against her life, and warned her that she must on no account change her mind and return to Kirk o' Field. Making no effort to conceal his movements, Bothwell went back into town, roused some of his own people, and led them to the Provost's House.

5. Either then or earlier in the day he met Balfour and compelled him to reveal what preparation he had made.

6. Bothwell saw his chance to take advantage of the double plot—the altered and subverted plot—by lighting the fuse

that had been intended to serve first a Catholic then a Protestant cause. If Darnley were removed the Queen would need another husband, and her husband would be the most powerful man in Scotland.

7. He set fire to the fuse. Darnley and his valet were killed by the unexpected power of the explosion, and Bothwell, contradicting public accusation by a show of force, compelled a helpless jury—though it was not a packed jury—to find him not guilty.

8. To establish in the land the power he desired, and that now was necessary for his security, he forced the Queen into marriage by capture and rape.

9. That the Queen had married under duress became evident in her continued unhappiness, and those who might have rallied to her were alienated from Bothwell. His assumption of power was resented by the greater part of the Scottish nobility, and when it came to trial at arms he was betrayed by James Balfour, to whom he had been compelled—by Balfour's threat of blackmail—to give command of Edinburgh Castle. Bothwell was defeated at Carberry Hill, the Queen imprisoned on Loch Leven.

10. Moray and the Protestant Lords were not yet safe in the authority they had won. Their rebellion could be justified only by their ability to prove the criminal association of Mary and Bothwell to murder Darnley. To prove this—and exculpate themselves—they concocted, with some clumsiness, the evidence of the Casket Letters.

11. As evidence, the Casket Letters are of no value, because the originals of those that were said to incriminate Mary were never publicly produced; there are manifest contradictions in them; the so-called sonnets are not the work of a woman whose gifted youth had been spent among poets in France; and the all-important Letter II is clearly not the missive of a single day but the compilation of fragments of a diary or patches of a memorandum and pieces of genuine letters written on unidentified occasions, joined and cemented by forgery and interpolation.

12. The value of the Casket Letters lies in their disclosure of the motives of those who concocted them, and sent to England Scots translations of the alleged originals with the ingenuous query: 'If the French originals are found to tally with the Scots translations will that be reckoned good evidence?' Or, in other words, 'Shall we have to doctor and decorate the so-called originals a little more convincingly?' Moray and Lethington, with their guilty knowledge of the counter plot that failed, concocted the letters for their own safety; and as confession of their guilt and fear, they are proof of Mary's innocence.

CHRISTOPHER SYKES

*The Murder of the Duke of
Enghien March 21st, 1804*

THERE is not much mystery as regards the facts of the murder of the Duke of Enghien. We know who murdered whom and under what circumstances. We know what the motives were. We know how the murderers and the victim behaved. Where, then, lies the fascination of this repulsive crime? To some extent in the fact that the actors in it bore famous names: the murderer-in-chief was Napoleon; his accessaries were Murat, Savary, and Caulaincourt, and his accomplice-in-chief was Talleyrand; the victim was the descendant of the Grand Condé and the last of his male heirs. Yet this murder was not merely a drama with a star-studded cast. I would say that its fascination lies in the fact that though there is nothing mysterious as regards the sequence of events, the event itself is highly perplexing from the psychological point of view. It was as though you had been warned that a homicidal maniac was about to break into your house; you load your pistol; you set out to catch him; you think you see him; you corner him—and then an informant in whom you have complete trust assures you that this is not the maniac, that you ought to be looking for somebody quite different, and you, instead of revising your plan, say, 'Oh well, I dare say this isn't the man after all, but here he is so I might as well kill him'; and you suit the action to the word. That is more or less what happened in the case of the Duke of Enghien.

He was called Louis Henri Antoine de Bourbon and was born in 1772 at the castle of Chantilly. He was the son of the Duc de Bourbon and grandson of the then Prince de Condé. The whole family emigrated after the fall of the Bastille, and in 1804 the Prince de Condé and his son were living in England, while the grandson, who bore the title Duke of Enghien, was living in Ettenheim on the German side of the Rhine and close to the river, in the electorate of Baden. The whole family were pensioners of the British government. As descendants of the Grand Condé they felt the indignity of their position, and in the case of the young man this seems to have taken the form of a frequent display of bellicose spirits. He was devoted to war; he had only one passion in life, he said, and that was to show himself on the field of battle as a soldier who was worthy to bear the name of his mighty ancestor. He sought to obtain a command in some army that would wage a campaign somewhere at some time against the armies led by those execrable rebels who had risen against the royal family of France. He looked upon himself as a patriotic Frenchman, and according to the ideas of the eighteenth century that is exactly what he was: how could you love your country and hate your King? How in 1804 could you serve Bonaparte as head of the French state while Louis XVIII was languishing in exile? Except as a traitor to France. The duty of a Frenchman was to draw the sword against Bonaparte and seize on the opportunity of war to force 'l'usurpateur', as the royalists usually called him, from his sacrilegious throne. From all accounts of the Duke of Enghien, by those who knew him, and from his letters, it is clear that he was of the extremest true-blue royalist cast of mind, and the fact that the French Revolution had awoken another form of patriotic mind was obviously something in which he did not believe and that he may not even have heard of.

The foregoing may suggest that he was just another of those privileged narrow-minded nonentities who had caused the fall of the old regime, discredited it in exile, and were to render its restoration in the years ahead futile and obnoxious. The truth was otherwise. Enghien was a worthy descendant of Condé. The aggressiveness of his opinions was in no sense the empty bombast of a fearful would-be soldier. In 1804 he had a

remarkable military record for a man of thirty-two. He had
fought throughout the campaigns of the royalist army under
his grandfather and he had obtained the devotion of his men
and the admiration not only of his superior officers but of his
French adversaries.

The royalist armies were easily demoralized, but this young
man had given them a new spirit, as reckless and daring as
that of the armies of Bonaparte himself. He asked to be put in
command of a vanguard at his first battle and led the charge.
A soldier of the French army had been heard to say after one
of his actions: 'But these aren't the old royalists—this is a
new sort. They fight like lions.' An Austrian general declared
that Enghien would have risen to high command even if he
had started in the ranks. A French general declared, '*Sa
bravoure, inutile d'en parler! C'était un Condé.*' Enghien was
the hope of the royal cause.

Enghien was not typical in mind of the emigrated aristo-
cracy. He was remote in character from the idiotic Count of
Artois who was the younger brother of Louis XVIII and the
incarnation of everything that was shallow and unreal in the
fallen monarchy. It was the custom of the French exiles, as of
all political exiles, to entertain absurdly optimistic hopes of
the impending fall of their adversaries and of the enormous
support that their cause enjoyed within their native country.
Enghien, on the contrary, had considerable political astute-
ness and he soon learned that the monarchy could only be
restored by means of a hard-fought war. It may have been
that he came to realize this by contact with Frenchmen of
France.

In 1799 he did a rash thing which could have cost him dear.
In the summer he went in disguise to Paris. These were the
last months of the Directory, when General Bonaparte was
still in Egypt. The Minister of War was Bernadotte and
Enghien succeeded in getting in touch with him. He put
forward a proposal that Bernadotte should bring Louis XVIII
back to France as King, and promised further that in the

event of a restoration Bernadotte would be made Constable of France. Bernadotte told him not to be naughty and gave him three days to leave Republican soil, which he did. News of this adventure reached his family and Louis. They were shocked and scolded him. He denied having gone to Paris— the only occasion on which he can be shown to have been guilty of an untruth—and he promised he would never do such a thing in the future. To his promise he was true. He continued to serve as a soldier.

When Napoleon became First Consul by the *coup d'état* of November 1799 royalists in France and outside let themselves believe that the new ruler's aim was to bring back the King; they remembered how General Monck had facilitated Charles II's restoration in England. Enghien saw the situation in its true terms. 'If Bonaparte restores monarchy in France,' he said, 'it will not be for the sake of the King, or the Count of Artois, or the Duke of Angoulême, but in order to place the crown on his own head.' He dedicated himself anew to the royal cause. Then his hopes received a final setback. On May 31st, 1801, the Army of Condé was finally disbanded as part of the general and short-lived peace of the early years of the Consulate. Chateaubriand described the occasion in a characteristic outpouring of sentiment: 'Now came the hour of separation. Brothers-in-arms bade each other a last farewell and then took their different ways over the face of the earth, none knowing where he might lay his head. Before leaving, every man went to salute his father and captain, the aged and white-haired Prince of Condé. The patriarch of glory gave his benediction to his children, wept over the dispersal of the tribe, watched the tents of his camp fall about him with the anguish of a father of a family who sees his ancestral roof crashing to the ground.' So life looked to a royalist in 1801, and Enghien felt the tragedy of the time. This was the end of his short and brilliant military career.

His grandfather and father went to England. He went to Ettenheim. His family wanted him to join them, but he insisted on making his home in this little Badish town. His reason was that he was in love with Princess Charlotte de Rohan-Rochefort. His family knew and disapproved: they wanted him to marry a royal princess, preferably a Russian grand-duchess, but he remained passionately and obstinately in love with Princess Charlotte, by all accounts a most admirable lady. She lived in Ettenheim with her father Prince de Rohan-Rochefort and her uncle Cardinal de Rohan, that dissolute and famous prelate whose infatuation with Queen Marie Antionette had brought about the Diamond Necklace Disaster. After the scandal the Cardinal had retired to his property at Ettenheim in order to repent and compose his soul. His last years were most edifying. He liked Enghien and encouraged him to marry his niece. In the end the lovers were married secretly in the winter of 1802–3, with the Cardinal's blessing and the lasting disapprobation of the royal family, the Prince of Condé, and the Duke of Bourbon. Few people knew about this marriage till many years later.

The Duke of Enghien lived in Ettenheim from September 1801 till within a few days of his death. His interests and conversation were found to be cultivated. He amused himself hunting in the forest country round about. Everyone who met him liked him. Modern taste may be somewhat repelled by his incessant longing for war and his reiterated insistence that he desired nothing but glory on the field of battle, but no impression of insensitiveness or boastfulness was recorded by anyone who knew him. What was undoubtedly attractive in his character was its openness. If he loved war he loved chivalry equally. He never repeated the adventure of 1799, which he probably regretted. He considered that a restoration by means of a plot would dishonour the throne, and he was profoundly shocked by any proposal for a counter-revolution achieved by terrorism. He was of the mind of Louis XVIII, who once said, 'In our family one *is* assassinated.' An illuminating thing in his character is that though he welcomed French deserters from the ranks he was dismayed by the desertions of commissioned officers, especially when these were the acts of men who had risen to high position or command under the Directory or the Consulate. Desertion by such men struck him as mean and ungrateful. He yearned to meet the paladins of the new France only on the field of battle where he would respect them. He was a man of candid and utterly simple mind. He was a warrior through and through.

Such was the victim. A young, handsome Prince, unhappy as all exiles are, conscious of wasted talents, living on hopes that he knew to be remote. Above all, he was a man of exemplary honesty, and in his childlike way he did not know that this is a somewhat rare quality.

The two main murderers were the most famous men in Europe: Napoleon Bonaparte, First Consul of the French Republic since Brumaire 1799, or the year VII; and Citizen Charles Maurice de Talleyrand, formerly Abbé de Perigord and Bishop of Autun. Which of the two was the prime mover in the murder is still open to debate. They were both accomplished liars, so the fact that the First Murderer, as one may call Napoleon, spoke about the matter on several occasions and at some length, blaming the Second Murderer at one moment and cheerfully acknowledging full guilt at another, does not signify as much as one would expect. Neither does Talleyrand's silence nor his later and then his posthumous voluble apology. It must be remembered that when he was head of the Provisional Government in Paris in 1814 Talleyrand spent a remarkably long time (when he could spare so little time as the Allied armies approached) in burning papers in the Ministry of Foreign Affairs. The evidence is established that the papers he burnt were those relating to the Duke of Enghien. Almost none were found after. It seems most likely that the First Murderer made up his mind to commit the crime, and that the Second Murderer found that the crime suited his book perfectly and so decided to give all the help he could.

One thing is very important to realize from the beginning:

the two men did not set out to commit a murder. On the contrary, they felt quite sincerely—at first—that they had no other object than to safeguard the French Republic from a recrudescence of the Terror, that state of bloody anarchy that was still fresh in men's minds and was the subject of frequent dread. They sincerely wanted to save France from a repetition of the horrors associated with the name of the semi-lunatic Robespierre. And it looked to them as though such horrors were preparing afresh.

The situation of Napoleon as First Consul was the most splendid, if not the most spectacular, that he occupied in the whole of his tremendous career. He introduced an age of tranquillity and energetic progress; France awoke from the nightmare of decadent monarchy, murderous revolution, and corrupt political systems. Even one of Napoleon's keenest and most unsparing critics, the Duke of Broglie, could say this of the Consulate: 'It was a deliverance, and the four years which followed its establishment were a succession of triumphs over external enemies and over internal anarchy. With the ten years of Henry IV's reign, those four years may be counted as the most glorious in French history.'

Most historians have subscribed to that opinion, but they have all been forced to acknowledge that through the triumphs and undoubted achievements of that great era there ran a dark thread. The evidence is that it came from a sense of insecurity. The men in authority were in a state of continual anxiety. They were running a compromise regime, and though this suited the majority, France was still well stocked with extremists. The personal position of the First Consul was more fragile than appeared. The eagle, glaring over the world, seemed the embodiment of self-confidence, but he had abundant reason for self-doubt, as all men have who have reached the heights of power through fraud. His return to France from Egypt in 1799 was a well-devised propaganda move based on exquisite distortion of the facts. He arrived as the Conqueror of the East, while, in fact, he had met a very considerable defeat in his Syrian campaign. He was acclaimed as the representative of the heroic French army which contrasted so magnificently with the shameful corruption and incapacity of the politicians of *Le Directoire*, but in fact he was a deserter who, seeing the game in the east was up, had hastened away from his men so as not to be hampered in his career by association with their failure. He appeared as the man of moderation, but the cruelty with which he had pursued the war in the east, notably his massacre of prisoners after accepting their surrender, had even turned the stomachs of his far-from-squeamish soldiers. In 1804 those soldiers were all back in France again; they had been coming back gradually all through the years of the Consulate; they might have a very different account to give of the victories achieved in the east by this wise and moderate man of destiny. Some of them were Jacobins who were not pleased by the semi-royal state maintained by the Consular regime. Others were beginning to look back nostalgically to the good old days of the King and Queen, and evidence began to accumulate that in eastern France dissatisfied soldiers had a way of glancing across the Rhine and wondering about the handsome, pathetic, and valiant young royal exile of Ettenheim. Occasionally men who deserted made their way there and would ask the young Duke to take them into his service. He was becoming something of a legend. The First Consul knew a good deal about legends and was the last man to underestimate their power. But during most of the Consulate he did not pay much attention to the legend of the young hero on the Rhine. It was not till the last year before the Empire that he gave royalism, as an explosive factor in the situation, any very serious thought. Then he veered round from contemptuous indifference to anger and alarm and panic.

Napoleon tended to exaggerate whatever was connected with royalty. He was never at his ease with this institution. He respected it, despised it, combined with it, and persecuted it, all to excess. He had had no career as a revolutionary worth speaking of, and this, with his continuance and enlargement of the Directory's policy of toleration, gave some people the idea that at heart the First Consul was a royalist. The royalist fancy that he wished to play to Louis XVIII the part of General Monck to Charles II had its origins in France. In fact, this idea, as Enghien came to realize, was very far from the truth. Napoleon was never a good republican at any moment of his career but he was never less of a royalist than in the years of the Consulate. It was a point of strong agreement between him and his Minister for Foreign Affairs, Citizen Talleyrand. Indeed, Talleyrand intensified this state of mind.

If Napoleon had nothing to gain by a restoration of the King, and probably much to lose, Talleyrand had literally everything to lose. His ambition was sleepless and for him politics was life. Once, in his old age, when the young Lamartine asked him whether he recommended politics as a career, he could only reply, 'But is there any other?' What political career could he have under a restoration of the Most Christian King, as a renegade aristocrat who had rejoiced over the execution of Louis XVI, and as a bishop who had abjured his orders? He would be lucky to escape with his life.

In the winter of 1802–3 he set his mind to make a restoration impossible. He laid his plans with great skill. On his initiative, and through the intermediary of the Prussian court, an offer was conveyed in February 1803 from the First Consul to Louis XVIII, then living in Warsaw, proposing that the King should renounce the throne on behalf both of himself and of his family, in exchange for which concession Napoleon would make him King of Poland and provide him with a generous indemnity. Talleyrand explained the essentials of his plan in the course of a conversation with Markov, the Russian ambassador in Paris. Markov wanted to know whether the French government would attach humiliating conditions to the indemnity. Talleyrand thought a while and then answered as follows: 'Acts of abdication are not valid according to the law as it was under the former monarchy, but what will give these acts the force of law is the debasement [*l'avilissement*] of the individuals concerned which will be complete in this instance,' an utterance which gives us a rare peep into the recesses of Talleyrand's amiable mind.

Louis XVIII, the fat, gouty brother of the late King, was a man of considerable parts. Unlike Louis XVI and his elegant and ridiculous younger brother Artois, he was a natural politician who in the remaining twenty years of his life was able to get things going his way in the face of ill-fortune, broken health, unpopularity, and hostility. He did not fall into the trap carefully prepared by Napoleon and Talleyrand. He had a genuine and impressive dignity and his answer to Napoleon's invitation to political suicide became famous in early nineteenth-century Europe. This was what he wrote to the intermediary: 'I do not make the mistake of confounding Monsieur Bonaparte with those who preceded him. I applaud his valour and his military talents. I am conscious of gratitude to him in consideration of several acts of administration, since deeds of benevolence towards my people will always be dear to me; but he is mistaken if he believes that he can draw me into negotiations whose purpose is to obtain my agreement to the diminution of my rights [*s'il croit m'engager à transiger sur mes droits*]. Far from that, he does but proclaim them himself, supposing that they could be the subject of legal argument, by the approach which he is making at this moment.'

If Louis had been so foolish as to accept the First Consul's offer then Talleyrand would obviously have achieved his aim. But the skill of this intrigue was that Talleyrand could be fairly sure of achieving it even if (as he must have expected) Louis had the sagacity to refuse the proposal.

Napoleon, as said already, was sensitive on the subject of royalty. It was part of his class-consciousness, a weakness one notes with surprise in so formidable a being. The weakness was very prominent, all the same, and it is no exaggeration to say that he was almost as class-conscious and as prone to worry about class matters as an Englishman of today. He could not bear to be snubbed by social superiors, either as a schoolboy or on St. Helena. And this pompous patronizing message of 1803 from a helpless fat elderly invalid in Warsaw was the most insufferable snub he had hitherto had to endure. Imagine the feelings of the man of destiny on being addressed by this ailing royalty as though he were a well-meaning, upper servant, whose promising efforts might lead him to quite a distinguished little career, if he would remember his station and not interfere in matters which were reserved to a very different class of person, his rightful employers in fact, who understood them! The rage of the First Consul was greatly increased when Louis obtained public approval of his reply from all the French princes. This was to make a public fool of the First Consul! Napoleon was reported to be particularly exasperated by the publication of a letter dated March 22nd 1803, from Ettenheim. It was addressed to Louis XVIII and read as follows:

'Sire,
    The letter with which Your Majesty has deigned to honour me has reached me this moment. Your Majesty knows too well what blood flows in my veins to allow of any doubt on Your Majesty's part as to what answer I will return to Your Majesty's request. I am a Frenchman, Sire, and a Frenchman who is faithful to his God, his King, and to his oath. One day perhaps many will envy me this three-fold advantage. May Your Majesty deign to allow me to add my signature to that of My lord the Duke of Angoulême, adhering like him in heart and in soul to the contents of the letter of my King.
                                Louis Antoine Henri de Bourbon'

After he had read that letter Napoleon began to include the young hero of the Rhine in his calculations. '*Dès ce moment*,' remarks Henri Welschinger, '*il fixa sur lui un regard menaçant*.'
    Talleyrand could now put aside any fears he may have felt at the remote possibility of a restoration. Things had fallen

out very well for him, but like the expert politician that he was he would not miss an opportunity of making assurance doubly sure, especially as he himself was sometimes suspected of secret royalism, not least by Napoleon, who was suspicious by nature and knew Talleyrand's remarkably broad capacity for turncoat betrayal. The opportunity came.

From one year after the foundation of the Consulate the French Government had been troubled by conspiracies. The first one was led by a Corsican who was called Aréna. The plot aimed to assassinate the First Consul at the opera. The police discovered the details and Aréna and his fellow conspirators were arrested on October 10th, 1800. Two months later another plot nearly succeeded. This occurred on December 24th and was known as the affair of the Rue Nicaise or of the Infernal Machine. The conspirators attacked Napoleon and Josephine with a bomb as they were driving in the Rue Nicaise near the Tuileries to attend the first performance in Paris of Haydn's *Creation*. They both escaped unhurt, but several people in the street lost their lives. Napoleon insisted that this was a Jacobin attempt and refused to listen to his Minister of Police, Fouché, when he told him that this was on the contrary the work of royalists. Napoleon stuck to his point. A hundred and thirty Jacobins were sent to tropical islands (whence only a few returned) and several prominent members of the outlawed club were guillotined.

In the spring of 1802 there was a mild anti-Consular demonstration in the army. It was restricted to propaganda and became known as "The Plot of the Placards'. It turned out to be of considerable importance. Once again Fouché informed Napoleon that this was a royalist outbreak, and once again Napoleon insisted that it was the work of rebellious Jacobins. Napoleon never trusted Fouché and did not forget that only some ten years before he had presided as a Jacobin over the reign of terror in Lyons. He suspected him of pretending that these plots were royalist in order to shield former associates of his guillotining days. His distrust led to a mistake fraught with consequences. He abolished Fouché's ministry and put the police under the Minister of Justice. To this post he appointed an eminent lawyer, the '*grand juge*' Claude Ambroise Régnier. In turn Régnier delegated police duties in his ministry to a Councillor of State, Pierre François Réal. The result of this reorganization was that in 1804 the First Consul was without first-rate police services such as Fouché knew how to organize. This was one of the origins of the murder.

During 1803 and in the winter of 1803–4 Napoleon came to revise his opinion about the relative dangers of Jacobins and royalists. The turning point seems to have been the miscarriage of his plans for the abdication of Louis XVIII, but his new irritation did not take fire till the beginning of 1804. There was a man hovering round Europe then called Mehée de la Touche who seems to have been one of the most remarkable double agents of whom there is record. Being in the confidence of the Count of Artois and many of the royalist leaders abroad, he was able to keep the Consular Government informed of the more extraordinary and hair-raising plans of the exiles. In return he gave the royalists much inside information about the French government. Like most spies, especially the self-employed sort, he dealt exclusively in exciting items of news. In January Mehée de la Touche was able to give his employers in Paris details of a proposal for royalist policy which had recently been submitted to Louis XVIII by a slightly dotty follower whose name was Bertrand de Moleville. This man had a plan for a secret alliance between royalists and Jacobins whereby the royalists should do nothing to interfere with Jacobin enterprises against the government of Napoleon, at the same time maintaining the hatred of the King's party against the Jacobins, and preparing to take over the government of France when the Jacobins would have caused the Consulate to fall by revolution, after which, presumably, the Jacobins would be liquidated in their turn. Napoleon and Talleyrand might have dismissed this nonsense from their minds if news of it had not been followed very shortly after by evidence of the greatest anti-Consular conspiracy to date.

This was led by a terrorist called Georges Cadoudal. He was famous as a fighter against the revolution from the very beginning, and he had a long record of gallantry and conspiracy. He had escaped from prison after the defeat of the Vendeans and eventually took to an underground life of intrigue. When things became too dangerous he went to England, but made frequent clandestine visits to France. He became famous in the country. Like many terrorists his superficial character was attractive, and he gained the reputation of a Robin Hood. Napoleon admired his energy and devotion to a cause, and early in his days as Consul conveyed an invitation to him to make his peace with the government and accept a post in the new France. But like most terrorists Cadoudal had a one-track mind. He refused. He was not in the least mollified by the First Consul's generosity. He was one of the moving spirits behind the Infernal Machine conspiracy shortly after Napoleon's offer of amnesty.

Sometime in August 1803 Cadoudal was known to be back in Paris, and furthermore he had come back with General Charles Pichegru, one of the most distinguished and sinister of the revolutionary generals. To a Frenchman who was not a royalist there were two names then that could only be pronounced with execration. One was that of General Charles François Dumouriez, the victor of Jemappes, the man who had saved the republic and had then later, after a reverse in 1793, fled in terror of the guillotine (it being the custom at the time to behead unsuccessful generals) in order to offer his services to Louis XVIII. The other name was that of General Pichegru, the victor of the revolutionary campaigns in Germany and the Low Countries, who in 1795, for no apparent reason other than innate treachery, entered into treasonable correspondence with the royalists. In 1798 he escaped from prison in a penal settlement and went to London. It is hard to say which of these men was considered the more perfect model for the role of the 'Enemy of the State'. Dumouriez was possibly less feared because he had no active partisans in the French capital. The same could not be said of Pichegru. He had a great friend in Paris, General Moreau.

This man had been the first to discover Pichegru's treachery, and out of friendship for an old comrade-in-arms he had concealed his knowledge till too late. Moreau remained under some suspicion, even after he had retrieved his good name in the field. He became embittered against the Directory and hastened to join Napoleon in 1799. Napoleon had taken him into high favour, but with disappointing results. Moreau married a friend of Madame Bonaparte, and this lady, unlike Josephine, was devoured with political ambition. Her salon became known as '*le club Moreau*' and was the meeting place of people who were becoming angry and disapproving at the First Consul's growing absolutism. Moreau, who never got rid of a feeling that he had been unfairly used, was not un-sympathetic to the hum of grumbling in his house. He re-garded himself as just as good a soldier as Bonaparte, and the latter regarded him as an ungrateful intriguer who was not to be trusted a yard. It became known that he had met Pichegru. On February 15th, 1804, Moreau was arrested. There was, however, no clear evidence against him, and from that day to this the question whether he was guilty or not has never been definitively decided.

Pichegru and Cadoudal remained undiscovered in Paris during the winter of 1803–4, though the police knew that they had been there since the summer. Fouché may have looked on with some amusement and professional dismay. In spite of his ejection from the government, the bulk of the information on the new conspiracy was collected by Fouché's agents, by a sort of private detective agency run by himself, but such an agency was no substitute for the Ministry of Police that Napoleon had suppressed in a fit of temper. The official police were clearly carrying out their duties inefficiently at a moment when news of a gigantic conspiracy, indeed of a new and bloody revolution, was daily to hand from agents such as Mehée de la

Touche, who operated a thriving spy-industry unhampered by the discipline of an efficient government department. With great difficulty Fouché kept the picture in some proportion.

Napoleon and those he consulted reached the conclusion that the leader and centre of the plot was the Count of Artois. In this they were correct, but with a difference. Artois had encouraged Cadoudal and Pichegru, and many others, but he was not the leader in the sense that he was prepared to cross over to France in the style of Bonnie Prince Charlie and lead his followers. He was not prepared to budge until the conspiracy had abundantly succeeded. The French government sent over *agents provocateurs* to persuade him to join Cadoudal, but they had no success, for Artois was decidedly against trying the hazard of war. He had attempted this once on behalf of the Vendeans in 1795, and found that it did not suit him. On that occasion, he sailed to the island of Yeu but refused to take the further step of landing in Brittany, and in the end sailed home in a British warship before the battle had really got going. Thinking about Artois gave Napoleon, Talleyrand, Fouché, and the rest a new idea. Surely the conspiracy must have some other and more active chief, besides the feather-brained, long-toothed playboy brother of Louis XVIII. Spies from the east told them that a large number of emigrants in Offenburg in Baden were conspiring furiously under a certain Madame de Reich. Offenburg is only about fifteen miles from Ettenheim. Their thoughts began to turn to the Duke of Enghien.

On February 28th the luck of the police turned. They found Pichegru in Paris and arrested him. It so happened that on the same day Mehée de la Touche arrived on one of his frequent visits from Baden. He had great news, all invented by himself. There had recently been a large and representative gathering at Offenburg, he said, attended by all the principal officers of the former *Armée de Condé*. The meetings had taken place at the house of Madame de Reich, and the central figure had been the Duke of Enghien. All this he reported to the Ministry of Justice.

It looked now as though the plot might break at any moment, so on March 2nd, as a first counter-move, Monsieur Réal sent an order to the Prefect of Alsace in Strasbourg, commanding him to find out all he could about the Duke of Enghien in nearby Ettenheim. On March 4th the Prefect entrusted a sergeant of mounted gendarmerie, *le maréchal des logis* Lamothe, with this duty. Lamothe was not another Mehée; he was a worthy, honest, hard-working police inspector, and the Prefect had no reason to doubt the sincerity or veracity of his report. He received it on the 5th. He immediately sent it by express messenger to Paris, to the chief of the gendarmerie service of France, General Moncey. The latter received the report early on March 8th. Its contents seemed to him of such significance that he requested an immediate audience of the First Consul. At eleven o'clock he was shown into Napoleon's study. He laid the report before him. One item threw all the rest into the shade. The Duke of Enghien had recently received two visitors from England, and these two were still at Ettenheim, for what purpose Lamothe did not specify. One of them was an Englishman called Lieutenant Smith. The other was General Dumouriez.

The whole outline of the conspiracy now appeared to be visible. While the Count of Artois stimulated the entry of agents into France from England the Duke of Enghien was organizing a rising in the eastern provinces of France. It was now quite clear why, when the rest of his family went to England, he chose to remain in dismal little Ettenheim. The pieces had fallen into place and the puzzle seemed to be solved.

Napoleon's first reaction to the news was entirely characteristic. He summoned citizens Réal and Talleyrand and gave them each one of those tremendous dressings-down of which he was said to be a master without compare. What, he demanded of Réal, in his merciless quick-firing manner delivered in crescendo, were the police doing allowing General Dumouriez to take up residence twenty miles from Strasbourg without their knowledge for purposes of a treasonable attack on the French motherland? Were the police in the conspiracy too? How else to explain this criminal delay? What was his answer? Had he got an answer? Don't keep the Head of the State waiting for an answer if there is one! Is there?

Monsieur Réal was not a strong man and his only object in life was to hold a good government post with the least friction between himself and his rulers. He got out of the present tempest by telling Napoleon that in his letter of March 2nd he had demanded full details from the Prefect of Alsace, but that he had not yet received the reply, for which reason he begged to be allowed to defer his own answer till he had heard from Citizen Prefect Shée. This was, in fact, a complete lie, as Monsieur Shée had written to Monsieur Réal by the same express post as he had used for Lamothe's report, and he had improved the occasion by giving an account, which he had probably heard from Mehée de la Touche or his like, of the clandestine visits to Strasbourg by the Duke of Enghien in the course of the last two years, all of which was without the smallest foundation. Monsieur Réal thought that he would keep this interesting information for some more propitious time. He judged rightly. Napoleon did not pursue the matter. It is permissible to suppose that he dismissed Réal with a scowl. He had bigger game in sight.

What, he demanded to know of Citizen Talleyrand, was the so-called Ministry of Exterior Relations supposed to exist for? To line Monsieur de Talleyrand's pockets with the bribes of foreign envoys? And what was all this talk about Monsieur de Talleyrand being the best-informed man in Europe when the most famous conspirator in Europe could take up residence with another conspirator against the Consulate within sight of the city of Strasbourg? And who in the name of the devil was the French representative in Baden? And who had appointed him? Who? Who?

Monsieur de Talleyrand, like Monsieur Réal, had recourse to a little bout of lying, but he did it more skilfully than the

Councillor of State and in a far-sighted manner. He agreed cordially with the First Consul that this was a perfectly calamitous turn of events. The conjunction of Dumouriez and young Enghien was nothing if not disturbing. The First Consul had mentioned the French representative at the Elector's court. He was called Monsieur Massias. The First Consul had intimated in his own very striking way that Monsieur Massias had been appointed by himself, Citizen Talleyrand. It was only too true. There was no doubt about it; he was culpable of the appointment, if fault there were. Hitherto all that Talleyrand had said was truth. Now he deviated from that path. The First Consul might not be aware, he said, that Madame Massias exerted a considerable influence over her husband. We do not know that he mentioned Madame Moreau, but she was certainly in both their minds at that moment. Talleyrand went on to say that Madame Massias before marriage had been called Böcklin, and that the Böcklin family were related to Madame de Reich. That, he insisted, might explain a great deal. Napoleon does not seem to have questioned the statement and fully accepted the explanation of his Foreign Minister. Of the latter on this occasion Henri Welschinger remarks: '*Que faisait un mensonge de plus ou de moins à Monsieur de Talleyrand?*'

The next day, on March 9th, the police had a really marvellous turn of luck. They surprised Georges Cadoudal as he came out of his place of hiding. There was a cabriolet chase through the streets between the Luxemburg palace and the Seine in the course of which Cadoudal shot one of his police pursuers dead. The chase ended with a street-fight in which Cadoudal was finally overpowered and captured. He was then interrogated. What he had to say was of extreme interest and agreed with what one of his associates who had been arrested with him told immediately after.

Cadoudal's story was briefly as follows: He was in Paris awaiting the hour when the conspiracy would move into action. The purpose was to seize the person of the First Consul but not to assassinate him, to kidnap him and remove him out of

France, after which Louis XVIII would return to Paris as the rightful head of the State. (This resolve not to assassinate Napoleon was not much believed then and is not widely accepted by historians today.) The hour to strike depended on the arrival of a certain 'Prince' in Paris. Cadoudal did not know his identity beyond the description of him as the 'Prince'.

Léridant, who was Cadoudal's associate, told the police that he had actually met this person in Cadoudal's house: he described him as a man of about thirty, tall, very distinguished in manner and dress, and he said he had been treated with much respect and as the leader of the whole attempt. Léridant, like Cadoudal, did not know who he was. The police thought they did: they jumped to the conclusion that this was Artois, in spite of the fact that Artois was nearer fifty than thirty. But when the police report reached Réal and through him went to Napoleon, Talleyrand, and Fouché, they were quite certain of the identity of this mysterious visitor to Paris. Artois would never dare undertake such travels, but Enghien would.

In fact the police were nearer the truth than their superiors. They had the advantage of not being stuffed with the bogus information which came to the people at the top. The 'Prince' was an emissary of Artois, Count Jules de Polignac. This was only known long after. With the arrest of Pichegru, Cadoudal, and Léridant, besides many others, the government could congratulate themselves that they had the conspiracy under some control. Now was the moment to turn that control into lasting and total victory in the true Napoleonic manner. Now was the moment to draw the sword and thrust it in deep, through the very heart of the opposition. The location of the heart was now no longer a matter for speculation but of reasonable deduction from a wide array of proof. It was in Baden. In the district of Offenburg and Ettenheim. Things now began to move fast.

The first initiative was a surprising one. Orders were issued by Napoleon and immediately conveyed to Monsieur Massias by Talleyrand to the effect that the French representative was to request from the Elector the arrest and extradition of Madame de Reich and the seizure of her papers. All this was carried out. Madame de Reich was placed under house arrest before being conveyed to Strasbourg, with the agreement of the Elector, an elderly, miserable, timorous, treacherous man who lived in hourly terror of the Eagle on the other side of the Rhine. What is odd about this move is that it could so easily have given the signal to flight to the man Napoleon was really after. The Duke of Enghien was in fact warned not by the Elector (he was probably shaking too much to write) but by a friend, the Marquis de Vauborel. Enghien was not perturbed. He was extraordinarily trusting. His reply to Vauborel is an important piece of historical evidence, as appears later.

The arrest of Madame de Reich took place on March 11th. This is to run ahead of the story by a day. On March 10th Napoleon called a Council of State which was attended by his two fellow Consuls, Jean Jacques de Cambacérès and Charles François Lebrun, by Talleyrand, Regnier, and Fouché. The meeting was led by Talleyrand, who described the elaborate network of royalist intrigue conjoined (according to the best intelligence) to Jacobin intrigue. He explained how it was operated partly from London, partly from Munich by English agents in collaboration with exiles, and how research had at last discovered its headquarters in Baden, presided over by the Duke of Enghien and the traitor Dumouriez. What action was to be taken? Desperate situations required desperate remedies, and Talleyrand informed the Council that in his submission the only sensible procedure was for a detachment of French military and police to enter the Electorate, surround Ettenheim, capture Enghien, Dumouriez and the English liaison officer Smith (to be treated thereafter as a prisoner of war), convey them to Paris, put Enghien and Dumouriez on trial for conspiring against the safety of the State, and then carry out the sentence of the court, which would be death. He was seconded by Fouché, who declared that unless a severe

example was made of the Bourbons immediately the conspiracies would continue because the royalists were being
perpetually encouraged by this lunatic idea that the First
Consul was planning to act the part of Monck.

It seems certain that the death of Enghien and Dumouriez
was discussed as something agreed on and to be accepted as
such from the curious revelation made ten years after by
Cambacérès. It appears that there was an interval in the
meeting, perhaps suggested by Cambacérès himself, and that
during it this Second Consul drew the First Consul aside. He
put it to Napoleon that he Cambacérès could not be suspected
of royalism, if only because he was known to have been one of
the judges of Louis XVI. He reminded Napoleon that on that
occasion he had urged a more clement sentence: delay of
execution until the end of hostilities, or until the invasion of
French territory, but that he had been overruled. In the end he
had voted for the immediate death sentence. Since then he had
been tortured, he said, by the thought that he had had a hand
in the death of an innocent man. 'I know,' he said to Napoleon,
'that in my innermost being I did not vote for that sentence of
death, but I bitterly regret and I will continue to regret to the
end of my days that I was numbered among the King's judges
and condemned him. Spare yourself remorse and regrets such
as I have had to endure!'

It is said that Napoleon replied to Cambacérès by saying:
'You have become very miserly of the blood of the Bourbons
[*bien avare du sang des Bourbons*]', but the Second Consul
asserted that he heard no such words from Napoleon. It is
probably a legend, but the legend indicates well enough that
Napoleon's mind was absolutely made up, and that no appeals
and no considerations were going to influence him. He had
come to close the revolution and open a new age. Neither
royalists nor Jacobins would stand in his way, least of all that
fat pompous pretender or the conspiring young hero of the
Rhine. He was a Corsican and the vendetta was in his blood.

On the resumption of the meeting (supposing that this is

how it fell out) there was a further objection from Judge
Régnier. The invasion of the Electorate of Baden was contrary to law, he protested. In such cases, replied Talleyrand,
where the safety of a great nation was at stake, international
law had to take cognizance of the fact that those who put
themselves outside the law could not claim its protection. He
added that the Elector of Baden was under heavy obligation
to the French government and that no trouble need be expected from him. The argument satisfied Régnier and when
the matter was put to the vote the First Consul obtained
unanimous agreement to the seizure of the Duke of Enghien
and his companions.

Here we see the beginning of one of the ugliest things in the
crime: the degradation under dictatorship of honourable men.
Cambacérès voted in spite of his scruples. What he said of his
inglorious part in the condemnation of Louis XVI applied
here: 'I voted as I could. I tried to soothe my conscience without
sticking out my neck [*sans trop exposer ma tête*]'.

Presumably the Council took place early on the morning
of the 10th. On the same day instructions were issued by
Napoleon to the Minister of War, Berthier. General Ordener
was to leave Paris and take command of a striking force
assembled in Alsace and consisting of three hundred dragoons
and thirty mounted gendarmes. The rendezvous would be the
ferry station of Rheinau. The second-in-command would be
General Fririon, commandant of Strasbourg. Ordener's objective was Ettenheim and the securing of the Enghien party.
A little later General Caulaincourt was to cross the Rhine
into Baden, also with a small mobile force, and make his way
to Carlsruhe in order to present explanations to the Elector
from the Ministry of Foreign Affairs. Caulaincourt was to
maintain contact with Ordener and the Ettenheim mission
and not to make diplomatic approaches to the Electoral court
until assured of the success of the expedition to seize the Duke
and Dumouriez. It was Talleyrand's idea to employ Caulaincourt on this mission. Caulaincourt was an aristocrat and

Talleyrand did not see why he himself should be the only aristocrat to risk his honour in the affair. Also, in the anti-royalist policy which he favoured at the moment, it struck him as a good thing to have this natural royalist thoroughly com-promised in a shady Republican undertaking. He had a great belief in *avilissement*.

Ordener left Paris on the 11th, Caulaincourt on the 12th. No one concerned doubted that this was an act of high-handedness that was hard to defend, but no one doubted that Enghien and Dumouriez were planning a disastrous subversion of the French State. No one was as yet out to commit a murder.

Then a little light began to filter through the fog of sham information which was surrounding the Consular Govern-ment. It came from Régnier. As a lawyer he was used to sifting evidence and as early as this he succeeded to a certain degree in sifting nonsense from fact in the case of Ettenheim. On March 12th he wrote to the First Consul a brief summing-up of the matter. He explained in his curious antique style and spelling that according to his information the Duke of Enghien lived at Ettenheim for the simple reason that he was in love. '*Il y vit avec madame de Rohan-Rochefort, dont il est depuis longtemps épris et dont la mère, vieille folle, est à Paris.*' Apart from his love affair, Régnier said, there was no other reason for the young man's protracted residence at Ettenheim. Régnier referred to rumours that some of the royalists in Paris had planned a rising at the head of which they would place not the pusillanimous Artois but Enghien and invite him to ascend the throne. Enghien, the judge reported, had laughingly dismissed such plans with the words: 'What are they thinking of? Count: I am tenth in succession. I am much too far off.' In brief, Régnier, by implication, urged the First Consul to reconsider his idea that Enghien was a desperately dangerous man.

Napoleon paid no attention to this letter, nor did Talleyrand. Régnier had not the courage to follow up his initiative, and things took their course. At the last moment Caulaincourt was given additional orders. Before crossing the Rhine into Baden he was to hold a meeting in Strasbourg so as to acquaint himself with the latest intelligence. He was to discuss the situation with the military there and with Monsieur Shée, and once again the name of Mehée de la Touche pops up in the story. Caulaincourt was to enrich his mind from that incomparable mine of misinformation. He was also to be certain to bring back the papers of Madame de Reich.

General Ordener arrived in Strasbourg on the night of March 12th–13th. After consulting General Leval, the divisional commander, and others, he did a remarkably foolish thing. In the early morning of the 13th he sent two policemen in plain clothes to make a last reconnaissance. The two of them were not gifted dissimulators, and after arriving in Ettenheim on the afternoon of the 13th they walked around the Duke's modest house with an ostentatious show of unconcern which drew attention to them. One of them seems to have been on this sort of duty before and was recognized by one of Enghien's servants as a member of the Strasbourg constabulary. The friends of the Duke urged him to leave Baden quickly. It so happened that the Elector's son-in-law, the King of Sweden, was on a visit to Carlsruhe, and he had heard all about the Madame de Reich affair. On the same day as these plain-clothes policemen pounded with affected innocence round the house at Ettenheim the King of Sweden sent to Enghien to urge him to leave Baden immediately. Princess Charlotte implored him to go too, now, while all was safe. He refused. He is said to have told those who warned him: 'They would not dare!' There may have been something more than over-confidence and bravado in his attitude. To have run away would not only appear cowardly (and Artois had left the House of Bourbon in need of some accent on courage) but could appear as a confession of his guilt as a conspirator with Pichegru who had made advances to him, and whom he despised.

On the 14th General Caulaincourt arrived in Strasbourg

and the two plain-clothes men, who were called Pfersdorff and Stohl, reported that the situation was satisfactory. He held his conference with the Prefect, General Leval, General Ordener, and Mehée de la Touche. In the late afternoon Caulaincourt left with the Prefect and Leval to go to Offenburg, meeting his troops at the ferry at Kehl, while Ordener left with General Fririon, to meet the force of three hundred and thirty dragoons and gendarmerie at the ferry of Rheinau.

Here a very strange thing happened. Fririon had not so far been let into the secret. At Rheinau he dined with a repatriated French exile called Monsieur de Stumpf. In the middle of dinner a messenger from Ordener came in with sealed orders for the General. He opened the packet, turned pale, rose from the table, and asked Monsieur de Stumpf to come with him into the next room. He told him what the orders were and how they shocked him. 'I was thrown into a state of violent agitation,' he told afterwards, 'by reading these orders which involved the violation of neutral territory and which for that reason alone struck me as outrageously unjust. And what did they want with the Duke of Enghien? To kidnap him as a hostage or rob him of life? Whatever the intention, here was an intolerable abuse of power and one calculated to stain with an ineradicable blemish the reputation of the French government whose power and prestige should have placed it above such brigandage.' (Interesting to note what a far firmer grasp of the nature of diplomacy was shown by this soldier than by Talleyrand.)

Unlike Régnier and others, General Fririon decided to act boldly according to his conscience. He asked Stumpf for help, and Stumpf thereupon wrote to the Mayor of Rheinau, who sent off his brother to warn Enghien of his imminent peril. He reached Ettenheim and got the message to the Duke around midnight. Still he would not leave, until it was represented to him by everyone in the house that this latest message could leave no doubt whatsoever of an impending attack and to stay was mere folly. At about four in the morning he agreed to go.

But by now it was too late. The cavalry under Ordener and his would-be saviour Fririon had surrounded the town, and presently they moved on to the house. He and his friends and servants armed themselves and prepared for a fight, but one of the older men in the house, Colonel Grünstein, urged the Duke not to resist, and seized his gun from him as he was about to shoot. 'Who commands here?' cried Enghien angrily, then saw that Grunstein was right. He told his people to put down their arms. A minute later the military broke in and, having arrested all the males in the house, led them away. They comandeered the whole premises and started a search for papers. There was a woman looking out of one of the top windows. She was in tears. Fririon's aide-de-camp shouted to her to ask which of the prisoners was the Duke of Enghien. She did not answer. She was Enghien's wife.

The whole party hurried back to the Rhine. Their first stop was at a windmill called La Tuilerie. Soldiers found a shop-keeper nearby and brought him to the place with threats to identify the chief prisoner. To prevent the poor man being ill-treated Enghien stepped forward and said, '*C'est moi qui suis le duc!*' They then wanted the names of all the prisoners and Enghien agreed that the names should be given. They were Colonel Grunstein, the Bavarian Lieutenant Schmidt, Abbé Weinborn, Abbé Michel, the Marquis de Thumery, and two servants called Ferron and Poulain. Where was Dumouriez? Where was Lieutenant Smith from London? Puzzlement equally on the part of captors and captured. The appalling truth began to dawn on Ordener and those of his officers who were in the great state secret of the hour. There was no Dumouriez. His name had been reported in mistake for that of the elderly Monsieur de Thumery who acted as Enghien's master of hounds and general *veneur*—easy mistake when his name was mangled by German peasant mispronunciation. There was no Lieutenant Smith from London. In so far as he existed he was Lieutenant Schmidt from Freiburg, a blameless officer of the Bavarian Elector. Enghien himself began to cease to exist as the legendary figure at the centre of the supreme conspiracy. The awful possibility stared everyone in the face that the First Consul might have made a mistake.

It is related that the swift journey back to Rheinau was made in depressed spirits. Enghien gave an impression of calm and resignation, though in fact he turned over in his mind how he might escape. A servant called Cannone who had escaped the arrest came on after with some clothes and linen for his master which he gave him at La Tuilerie, and was then allowed to accompany him on the journey to Strasbourg. With Cannone he planned to rush from the cavalcade and hide in the woods when an opportunity arrived, but it did not. He was amazed at the speed with which French cavalry moved and said, 'If I had known how fast you move I would have flown in time.'

During the journey there was some discussion of the case. Enghien asked the two generals how they were able to justify the invasion of neutral territory in order to seize a man whose interests were entirely private. Ordener was silent, but Fririon answered: 'Monsieur le duc, you are a soldier and you know that we cannot pass opinions on the orders we receive, no matter how painful they may be.' There was some general conversation in which some of the other officers joined in. Enghien was asked about Dumouriez and he answered that if this man had come to Ettenheim he would have turned him away, 'it being beneath the obligations of his rank to have to do with such people'. One of the officers said frankly that the Duke was suspected of being a party to the conspiracy of Pichegru and Cadoudal. Enghien protested with vigour, saying that he was utterly opposed to terroristic bids for power. 'Projects of that kind,' he said, 'are completely foreign to my view of life and my way of thinking. I will be frank and tell you how I stand. In spite of the fact that I admire the glory achieved by General Bonaparte, I have no alternative, as a prince of the House of Bourbon, but to make war against him whenever occasion offers.'

At four o'clock in the afternoon of March 15th the party arrived in Strasbourg. Shortly after this Caulaincourt arrived with a handsome clutch of male and female prisoners from Offenburg, Kehl, and Strasbourg itself, and the papers of Madame de Reich. He had sent a subordinate officer to Carlsruhe with the letter of explanation to the Elector, who was only too happy to receive it. The papers of Madame de Reich and of Enghien were immediately examined in the citadel of Strasbourg. Colonel Grünstein asked Enghien whether there was anything compromising in them. He replied: 'Nothing at all. The papers will confirm what is known already, that I am a soldier who has born arms during the last eight years and hopes to bear them again.'

From the 15th to the 18th the Duke of Enghien was lodged in the citadel of Strasbourg. He was allowed to write to Princess Charlotte whom he addressed on the cover by her maiden name as usual. He said that he was being treated with respect and consideration, urged her to put his case to the Elector, warned her not to do anything rash, above all not to try to follow him and thus endanger herself as well. As for the reasons for his capture he was as yet uncertain. 'They are looking for Dumouriez', he wrote, 'who appears to be somewhere in the district and they thought that I had had some consultations with him. He is said to be implicated in the plot against the First Consul's life.' In talking with his friends and the commandant he appeared to believe that he was going to be held in prison as a hostage, and looking round the walls of the citadel he wondered how he would be able to endure a life of confinement.

When the affair was over many of those concerned followed the example of Napoleon and Talleyrand, and were at pains to provide false accounts of what had happened, to change dates on papers, to lay false trails. It was not till 1888 that the researches of Henri Welschinger were able to show the sequence of events with any certainty. Even now there are gaps and question marks, but the main sequence is beyond serious doubt:

On the 15th, when the papers had been rapidly examined, the more interesting of them were sent direct to the First Consul and reached Paris on the 17th. Napoleon read them and sent them to Talleyrand on the same day. By then all the papers, with those of Madame de Reich, had been thoroughly examined in Strasbourg and were sent, with a written statement by Enghien, to Napoleon in Paris, where they arrived on the nineteenth or early on the 20th. In the meantime Enghien had been set on his way to Paris. It was now that he saw for the first time the extent of his peril. New orders had been received from Napoleon. The Duke was awoken at one o'clock in the morning of March 18th and told to get dressed. When he was ready he was taken down to where a coach drawn by six horses was waiting with a small cavalry escort. He was told that he was to travel under the name of Monsieur Plessis. His servant Cannone came with a few things, but as he was about to follow Enghien into the carriage the guards pulled him back and thrust him away with blows of their muskets. Enghien shouted to him, 'Go back, Joseph, and remember I am grateful to you.' While this scene was going on Enghien's dog, a Russian pug called Mohiloff, scampered between the legs of the soldiers and dashed into the carriage. The officer in charge of the convoy, Lieutenant Peterman, ordered that the dog might stay. He was the only friend allowed to accompany Enghien in his last days. With the astonishing speed of French horse-travel of those days they set off.

In Paris the government had to face an awkward situation. The great conspiracy against the First Consul had been wholly outmanœuvred and suppressed by the arrests of Pichegru and Georges Cadoudal. It was realized too late that this was the fact and that the reports of an Enghien plot had been an otiose absurdity. As an innocent man captured in the course of a monstrous violation of law he was now a most inconvenient object. If only he had obliged by being guilty then the whole incident was open to defence. As an innocent man it was very difficult to know what to do with him. To send him back again to

Baden would make the Consular Government look utterly ridiculous. There was, however, no question of returning him home. Napoleon was in the Corsican mood. He had not forgotten that patting-on-the-head letter of Louis the Fat, and here in his hands he held the hope of royalism. He gave a Corsican explanation of his feelings: 'I had done nothing against them. They had no right to conspire against me.'

Admirers of Napoleon have drawn a picture of the First Consul in a state of divided mind, ignorant of royal and royalist French affairs, and in this instance guided solely by Talleyrand. No one admired Napoleon more than himself and he originated this version of the story. It was on that famous occasion when he returned to France from Spain to upbraid Talleyrand and Fouché for plotting against him and when the Emperor, among other endearments, publicly described Talleyrand as a lump of *merde* in a silk stocking. In the course of that interesting conversation he exclaimed: 'And what about the wretched Duke of Enghien? Why, until you came with your conspiracies and libels I had never heard the man's name!' This gives neatly what might be called the Left Wing version of the affair: Honest Bony led astray by the slimy aristocrat Tally. There is not a particle of truth in the picture.

Even if Napoleon were late in becoming 'Enghien-conscious', he had certainly known all about him since March 1803 when he published that exasperating letter to Louis XVIII. It can be agreed that the orders to seize Enghien were given under a genuine belief that he was engaged in a terrible conspiracy. But Napoleon knew by the 17th in part, and by the 19th fully, that the conspiracies of Offenburg and Ettenheim were nonsense, and that Dumouriez was in no way connected with Enghien. This he knew, not from Talleyrand, but from examination of the papers. He was the First Murderer.

Then there is the other story. Admirers of Talleyrand assert that though as Foreign Minister he may have been stampeded by misinformation into approving the raid on Ettenheim, he later sought in vain to set the matter to rights. The wise states-man, it is said, was baulked by the brutal man of war. This also is empty myth. The initial responsibility appears beyond doubt equal between Napoleon and Talleyrand. When the First Consul turned anti-royalist Talleyrand made sure that his fury was maintained at white heat. He spotted the point on which pressure needed to be applied, the letter of Louis XVIII. In his communications before the deed he was careful to apply the goad: he reminded Napoleon of the name of Monck. It never failed to exasperate. It was Talleyrand who led the Council on March 10th. As with Napoleon, it can be argued in his favour that he really did believe that Enghien was plotting with Dumouriez. But after the 17th and the 19th?

Talleyrand was much cleverer than Napoleon. He was not a Corsican for one thing; he hated the old royal regime as much as, and probably more than, Napoleon, but he had no personal vendetta passions to cloud his vision; he could play it cool. As regards information, he was better furnished than Napoleon; he not only had Enghien's papers to prove the man's innocence, on the 17th and the 19th, but in addition (what Napoleon had not) he had a despatch from that same Monsieur Massias whom he had been at such pains to calumniate. On the day that he heard the news of the abduction Massias wrote to Talleyrand by express post and the letter must have certainly reached him before the 20th. 'Voluminous information has come to me', he wrote, 'on the character of the Duke of Enghien. It is to the effect that he is a royalist of the most ardent fidelity, a man who has no love for England and is humiliated at having to live on a pension. He is forced to live very economically and supports several people more unfortunate than himself as best he can with his straitened means. He is not a man made for intrigue. He is opposed to all cowardly action and abhors the terrorists. This information does not come to me from the court or courtiers. I have had it since long before there appeared any need for it, and it comes entirely from disinterested

persons. If it turns out that the papers in the hands of Judge
Régnier prove a case against this man, then I can only say that
error has made the impression on me that only truth should,
and that to the former Duke's tendency to intrigue and
cowardliness you must also add the most detestable hypocrisy.
I know, Citizen Minister, that if I had failed to communicate
this I would for the rest of my life feel that I had failed in my
duty.' And what did Talleyrand do with this information?
Nothing. He showed it to no one. He hid it. It was forgotten
for more than eighty years. He was playing it cool. Napoleon
was acting along the lines that Talleyrand approved, so he
astutely did not unsettle him with disturbing novelties, or
even too much with his own presence. From now on Talleyrand
kept in the background. He calculated that the murder would
be committed without his stir, and that if he did not stir, then,
if there should be revulsion at the killing of an innocent man,
he would all the more easily be able to slither out of responsibility. This is not mere guess-work. There is documentary
proof that within a few weeks of the deed he was arranging for
friends to concoct a convincing and wholly fallacious account,
very flattering to himself, of the process of the Enghien
affair. He continued to calumniate Monsieur Massias in a
quiet and telling manner. People who see in Talleyrand one
of the great men of history must admire all this too.

In the afternoon of March 20th the coach conveying the
Duke of Enghien and his guards, with the cavalry escort,
arrived in Paris. They drove straight to the Ministry of Justice
in the Rue des Saints Pères. From here they were directed to
the Ministry of Foreign Affairs in the Rue du Bac. One sees
already some anxiety to pass this inconvenient object from
hand to hand. In the courtyard of the Foreign Ministry they
were kept waiting while their arrival was reported within.
Enghien's spirits are said to have risen. He had an idea that he
was to be taken for an interview with the First Consul, in
which case he was sure that he could convince him of his
honourable position. Presently halting footsteps, as of a lame

man, were heard coming down the interior staircase, through the hall, out into the courtyard, into a carriage which immediately drove off. The last thing Monsieur de Talleyrand wanted was to see his victim. In this he was at one with Napoleon, who had driven off to Malmaison on the 12th to spend the next few days there, out of reach of petitioners. Orders which had been left by Talleyrand were given for the Duke of Enghien to be driven off to the fortress of Vincennes. They arrived there towards sunset at half past five.

The First Consul had made all arrangements through Monsieur Réal, the Ministry of War, and the Governor of Paris, who was his immensely over-dressed brother-in-law, General Joachim Murat. On Réal and Murat rested responsibility for carrying out the final orders.

Murat had been on and off stage since the 10th, but he made his first dramatic entry on the day before Enghien's arrival in Paris, on March 19th. The circumstances were curious and were such as to suggest to some that he was the driving force behind the crime, but in fact this was a long way from the truth. There was nothing of cruelty or revengefulness in Murat. His role brings out quite different qualities. Underneath the gorgeous laced uniforms, the glistening ringlets, the jewels, feathers, and elaborate oriental swords and pistols of Murat, there was a simple, well-meaning, and far from confident or strong character. He was the last man to want to commit murder off the battlefield. The reason that his role appeared sinister is perhaps because Napoleon sought an alibi through him. Certainly Napoleon's behaviour on the 19th remains perplexing.

Since the 12th he and Joséphine had been at La Malmaison with the Consular staff, and with Madame de Rémusat as Joséphine's *dame d'honneur*, for already the Consular household was putting in practice for when it would be an imperial court. Madame Bonaparte seems to have known about the expedition to Ettenheim from the beginning and early on in the affair she had implored her husband to show mercy. He had

replied by giving her a characteristic lecture on the mis-
chievousness of women in public affairs and had emphatically
refused the plea. He said: 'My policy requires a *coup d'état*.
A death which can ensure the tranquillity of the country is no
crime.'

On the evening of the 19th, after dinner, Napoleon asked
Madame de Rémusat to sit down to a game of chess. While
they were playing he recited snatches of his favourite poet
Corneille. Several times he murmured, '*Soyons amis Cinna.*'
She also knew about the abduction and the idea came to her
that Napoleon was referring to Enghien. She exchanged glances
with Joséphine. And then her hope that Napoleon was con-
templating a great and dramatic act of mercy became a certainty when he repeated the lines from Voltaire's Alzire where
Guzman declares that his faith compels him to show forgiveness even to the man who would slay him:

> '*Et le mien quand ton bras vient de m'assassiner
> M'ordonne de te plaindre et de te pardonner!*'

He said the lines over and over again. Madame de Rémusat
looked at him boldly. He returned her astonished stare and
smiled. Visitors were announced. Napoleon abandoned the
game and went into his study, where he remained till a late
hour. His visitors were Murat, General Savary, and General
Hulin. It was the conviction of Joséphine that Murat altered
her husband's mind.

In fact the wretched Murat tried as hard as he could to dissociate himself from the crime, but as hard as he could was
not nearly hard enough. The original plan was to hold a
grand state trial before a public tribunal. This arrangement
had to be quickly abandoned when discovery was made of the
prisoner's innocence, that continually exasperating and complicating factor. The state trial would have been a big set-
piece, but it was necessary to avoid all publicity in the case of
a trial where there could be no defence counsel. As military

Governor of Paris, Murat was responsible for lodging the prisoner, finding the necessary guards, and so on. To none of this he objected while he assumed that there would be a trial under normal legal procedure, but when he found that a very different form of trial was intended, and why, and that he was now responsible for putting together the instrument of in-justice, for selecting the 'military commission' charged with examination, condemnation, and execution, then his straight-forward soldierly mind and soul rebelled.

In spite of the late-night session in Malmaison, Murat was not told precisely what was expected of him till the morning of March 20th. He immediately went back to Malmaison and a stormy interview with his brother-in-law. Napoleon threatened to demand his resignation from the army and to banish him 'to his native mountains' if he dared to disobey his latest orders. But though the conversation was angry it did not cause a breach. Murat went back to his headquarters in Paris, where he found the brother of the Minister of War, Berthier, with a request that he would constitute the military commission. He refused. At four o'clock Réal called and told him that the prisoner had arrived and, on the First Consul's instructions, was on his way to Vincennes. At seven o'clock General Savary arrived with a letter from Napoleon which formally instructed him to convoke the Commission and gave details as to whom he wished appointed. Then Murat collapsed and signed the deed for calling together this bogus court-martial. He decided, after all, to do what was asked of him.

This is to run ahead somewhat.

In the morning of March 20th a Council had been held in the Tuileries Palace. The three Consuls attended and among the ministers was Judge Régnier. It is clear from the official record that policy was to keep the Enghien affair in the back-ground for the moment. Amid a mass of minor legislation, such as that concerning a legacy to a hospital, an entry is to be found for this day mentioning that, relative to orders issued already regarding the '*conspirateurs qui s'étaient réunis*

dans l'électorat de Bade . . . le ci-devant duc d'Enghien' was
to appear before a military commission to answer certain
charges. The priority of the charges was stated. Number one
was 'having born arms against the Republic'; number two
was 'having been and still being in the pay of England';
number three and last was 'being party to the plots engineered
by this last-mentioned power against the internal and external
security of the Republic'. Judge Régnier, who had been the
first to warn the First Consul that the major charge might be
empty, raised no further objection at this Council, now that his
opinion had been proved correct.

In the afternoon of March 20th Major Harel, the commandant of the fortress, received Enghien at Vincennes. Three
days before, he had been warned to have a room ready in the
Pavillon du Roi for a prisoner whose name was not given. On
the 20th Réal sent him a further message. 'The instruction of
the government', this read, 'is that the utmost secrecy shall be
observed regarding this prisoner. You alone are to communicate with him and you are not to permit him to speak to
anyone else until the receipt of further orders from me.' The
coach containing the prisoner arrived a few minutes after this
letter.

Harel was a rough soldier who in earlier days had been a
strong Jacobin. He had been an anti-Bonapartist in 1799 and
was reduced in rank after the establishment of the Consular
regime. However, it had become known that when the various
conspirators had made advances to him to enlist his aid he
had remained loyal, so as reparation he had been promoted
back to the rank of major and put in charge of the ancient
fortress and prison. He seems to have been a decent sort of
man, another of those who were degraded into a horrible
deed by the force of tyranny. His first care was to make his
prisoner reasonably comfortable. He knew who he was.

Enghien arrived looking pale and worn-out. He was wearing
a long blue riding coat and a peaked hunting cap of the same
colour ornamented with gold lace. Harel took him up to the

room that he had prepared and lit a fire for him. Enghien looked eagerly out of the window at the forests which he had not seen for fifteen years, and he told Harel how he remembered coming here as a boy and being shown the rooms where the Grand Condé had been lodged in the days when he was a state prisoner of Louis XIII. Harel arranged for his sergeant to fetch a dinner to his own room from outside. He took Enghien to his own more comfortable lodging. The sergeant, who was called Brigadier Aufort, left an account: 'I offered excuses for the poor fare which was all that I could succeed in getting in the town. The prisoner accepted my apologies with great good humour. He said he was perfectly satisfied, that a simple meal was all he wanted and he thanked me for the trouble I had taken. Just as he was about to take some soup, he turned to Harel who was standing a little behind him. "Monsieur," he said, "I have something to ask. I have with me my companion of the journey, the only friend from whom I have not been separated: that little dog that you see there. I hope you will not think that I am dishonouring your dinner if I share it with him. The poor creature has had little to eat since Strasbourg and I want to show him some gratitude." I was sorry to have brought so little and I promised to bring him a better dinner next day. Alas, I had no idea that this was to be his last meal.'

After dinner he asked Harel: 'What do they want? What do they want to do with me?' Harel gave evasive replies and showed considerable embarrassment. His wife overheard the conversation from the next room and could hardly control her emotion. By an extraordinary coincidence Madame Harel and Enghien had been nursed by the same foster-mother. But that was not the only reason for her and her husband's distress. In the afternoon a message had come from Savary, anticipating instructions from General Murat, ordering Harel to prepare a grave in one of the courtyards. The paved ground within the fortress courtyards was found impossible for this purpose if the grave was to be dug quickly, and hurry was the essence of the deed. So the commandant had ordered a grave to be dug in the moat. It was being dug at that moment.

After a little more talk Harel conducted the prisoner back to his room. There he undressed, lay down, and went to sleep.

It was now about seven o'clock, the moment when General Savary arrived at Murat's house with Napoleon's order for the formation of the military commission. The last paragraph of the order read as follows: 'You will make the members of the Commission understand that this business must be finished this night, and you will order that if the sentence is, as I cannot doubt it will be, one of condemnation to death it will be carried out immediately [*soit sur-le-champ executée*] and the condemned buried in one of the courtyards of the fortress. I command Savary to place himself at your disposal. He will himself detail what soldiers and officers of his legion will compose the two detachments [to take post at Vincennes] and he will supervise the entire operation [*veillera sur le tout*].'

Groaning in spirit, Murat appointed the Commission. The chairman was to be General Hulin, at Napoleon's specific request. The rest who were chosen by Murat in conformity with the First Consul's general indication were called Colonel Guiton, Colonel Bazancourt, Colonel Rarier, Colonel Barrois, Colonel Rabbe, Captain Dautancourt, and Captain Molin. The only appointment made by Napoleon, that of General Hulin, is interesting. He was known to hold Jacobin opinions and (according to Boulay de la Meurthe, who gives a somewhat favourable view of Napoleon's conduct) was chosen as being a person most unlikely to take a merciful view of a royal personage facing grave accusations.

The members of the Commission came to Murat's house one after another as they received their summons. They were not all assembled there till nine o'clock. Murat could not face a meeting with them, and, claiming that he was ill, stayed upstairs in his room. His aide-de-camp came down and gave the commissioners their instructions. Savary went up for a word with him and on the staircase met Talleyrand. From now on the Citizen Minister for External Relations was remaining in the background, but he had paid a visit to the First Consul earlier, and evidently thought that a word in season might be of advantage here. They say that a watched pot never boils, but that is no argument for paying no attention to the pot whatsoever. Murat, in affliction of soul, continued to carry out the First Consul's orders.

While the members of the Commission were assembling at his house Murat had signed the order for the movement of troops, presumably at Savary's request. Forty *gendarmes d' élite* and sixty men drawn from the garrison of Paris were to move on Vincennes. They reached there soon after nine o'clock. About an hour after this Murat received a visit from the chief of Napoleon's secretariat, Hugues Bernard Maret, better known by his later imperial title, the Duke of Bassano. He told Murat that the First Consul had sent a detailed interrogatory to Réal and suggested that possibly it might be beneficial if Hulin had an interview with Réal and Judge Régnier, though he did not think this necessary. His next remark suggests that Napoleon had sent the interrogatory to provide a show of justice, if anyone wanted one later, and that he preferred the judges to act without the cumberance of this or any other documentation. Maret worshipped Napoleon as a god and he would never have dared to contradict his orders or even faintly to misrepresent them, yet what he said to Murat was as follows: 'For the rest, the decree [passed at the Consular meeting in the morning] which defines the charges seems to me a sure guide to reaching the required sentence.' This was manifestly Napoleon's message.

The decree in question occupied about a hundred and twenty words and was the only document given to the judges relative to the case. It cited no evidence but merely contained statements of accusation, no more. The large collection of Enghien's letters made by the raiding parties at Ettenheim and Offenburg was not open to the commissioners' inspection. This at first seems odd, since the letters did contain one item which with only a little forensic skill could be made very damaging to Enghien's case. In writing to the British chargé d'affaires in Vienna, Sir Charles Stuart, Enghien had said that there were a number of deserters from the French army and he was prepared to form these into a unit to fight in the war. This was as near as Enghien came to the sort of intrigue he was accused of. Why not show it to the Commission? It is clear why it was not shown. It would raise the whole question of Enghien's bearing arms against France. In the captured correspondence it was related that he had once sought to hold a commission in the English army and that he had been refused on the plea of his father and grandfather. The Duke of Bourbon had written to him to say that it was beneath the dignity of a Condé to serve in a foreign army and the young man had repented. All this was in the letters. He had only born arms in the *Armée de Condé* and if this deserved death then there were thousands of returned emigrants who ought by rights to suffer with him, and the plan was not to open a new reign of Terror but to accuse Enghien of attempting this. The letters also disposed of any notion that Enghien was concerned in the Cadoudal-Pichegru conspiracy. His reply to the Marquis de Vauborel had been picked up in Offenburg. It ran as follows:

'I know, my dear general, that measures have been taken to spy on those in receipt of an English pension and especially on myself. I have been warned since a long time. But I can assure you that the fear of meeting some wretched hireling of a spy will not influence my actions in the very least. It is believed that my letters are opened. If that is so, I do not regret it as thereby men may understand my point of view and way of thinking, and how much and how continually I disapprove of our cause being served by methods which are unworthy of it, methods which have already done it so much harm, and I hope that the recent arrests in France [of Pichegru and his associates] will rid our cause of semi-converts who can do nothing but damage to it.'

It was obvious folly to give the Commission even a particle of a correspondence which contained such letters, for no matter how carefully the selection of pieces was made, question and answer might lead the enquiry into obvious evidence of this man's innocence. No one, not even Napoleon, knew about his visit to Paris in 1799. Bernadotte kept his word that he would take no action. If they had known the case would have been conducted quite differently. As it was, the Commission was given as the brief for the prosecution a slip of paper on which a hundred and twenty words were written. To make absolutely sure, Savary was there to see that no one strayed from the ordained path.

Slowly those who had set this crime in motion withdrew. Napoleon remained at La Malmaison where the atmosphere was oppressive, silent, hateful. Joseph Bonaparte had made the last intervention on the grounds that when they were boys the Condé family had shown the two brothers some kindness. Napoleon quietly told him to mind his own business. The mission of his chief of secretariat Maret to Réal and Murat was his last personal move in the affair. Talleyrand had written to the French ambassadors abroad telling them to defend the affair as a necessary act of self-defence and to reject 'avec moquerie' protests about the violation of territory. He had felt the pulses of his collaborators and now had nothing further to do. According to the account of a reliable contemporary, Vitrolles, he passed the night in cards and conversation at the house of a lady called the Vicomtesse de Laval. Murat had acted his part. Henri Welschinger said: 'He did what was asked of him with hesitation, with regret; that is certain. But he did it. He protested, but he signed.' Fouché had retired from the scene altogether after the Council of March 10th. He had one overriding interest in the outcome of the affair, to obtain a revival of the Ministry of Police. He waited outside Paris in his country house. The last scene was dominated by General Savary, a brilliant soldier and a man of ugly severity of character. He was the least attractive of the hard, gifted men who surrounded Napoleon. He was an embodiment of obedience. A man had to be murdered. Right. He would see that the murder was carried out. That was how he saw it.

Captain Dautancourt was chosen for the role of Captain-Advocate. He went with three officers and two gendarmes to Enghien's room at eleven o'clock, and awoke him. Dautancourt then undertook an examination in conformity with instructions given to him in Murat's house. He began with a formality, the Duke's name, and first name, age, and so on. Then he got down to questions. First his movements in detail since 1789. The prisoner gave them. Then an explanation, please, of his residence at Ettenheim—he said that he lived there with the permission of the Elector. Money from England —he explained that he had been granted a pension from the British government and this was his only source of income. Who did he write to? His father and grandfather chiefly. Now what about his relations with Pichegru? He replied as follows: 'I have never seen him and have had no relations of any kind with him. I know that he wanted to see me. I am glad to say that I never met him, especially after the horrible things that people say he wanted to do, assuming that what they say is true.' Well what about Dumouriez? He replied that he held Dumouriez in the utmost contempt. The examination was not going very well. Dautancourt returned to the question of his correspondence. Was it not true he had written to people in France? Yes, it was true, but he had only written to them about family affairs. That was the last question in the examination.

A minute of the proceedings had been taken. Enghien made a request that he might be allowed to add a statement in writing. This was agreed and he added the following:

'Before signing the present minute [*procès-verbal*] I make, with insistence, a request that I may be granted a personal interview with the First Consul. My name, my rank, my way of thinking [*façon de penser*], and the horror of my situation make me hope that he will not refuse my request. L. A. H. de Bourbon.'

Dautancourt returned to his colleagues, who were assembled in one of the central halls of the fortress. He read his account of the examination. It was now nearly one o'clock in the morning and the Commission decided, in conformity with the orders that had been transmitted to them by Murat, to hold the trial immediately. So as to keep up the appearance of legality, a few people were allowed in so that it could not be said that the prisoner was tried in secret. Some of the officers attended and a few men and women who were employed in the great château. The prisoner was brought in, and the official report expresses it thus: 'The president of the court caused the accused to be brought in free and unbound [*sans fers*], and then instructed the Captain advocate to acquaint the court with documents relative to the prosecution and defence, *to the number of one.*' This single solitary one was the piece of paper bearing the decree of the Consular meeting that morning. None of the commissioners had ever served in any capacity in any sort of court before this night. Even so, one might expect that someone would have protested at a trial on a capital charge being based, as to prosecution and defence, on one document alone. No one did. Behind General Hulin's chair stood Savary.

Dautancourt read the minutes of the examination. The prisoner was then asked for a statement. According to the record of Hulin: 'He rejected energetically the accusation of having taken any part, either direct or indirect, in the plots to assassinate the First Consul. He insisted that he had upheld the rights of his family and that a Condé could never come back to France except with his sword in his hand. My birth and opinions, he said, must always make me the enemy of your government.' Hulin went through the questions of the examination and Enghien replied as he had done before, laying particular stress on his repugnance to taking part in any kind of conspiracy. Hulin then put the following question to him:

'How will you persuade us that you were as ignorant as

you say of what was happening in France when all this was well known not only in the country where you were living but throughout the whole world? And how could you have remained indifferent to these events, given your birth and rank, when the results for yourself were so manifestly important? Be careful how you answer for this is a serious question and a military commission judges without appeal.'

According to Hulin's own record, written with an eye to self-defence, Enghien's reply was somewhat compromising. He is reported to have said: 'I can only repeat what I have said before. Hearing that war had been declared, I applied for a commission to serve in the armies of England, but the English government answered that they could not grant me a commission but that I should remain on the Rhine where I should soon have a part to play, and I waited accordingly.' What is suspect about this version of his answer is that in spite of it telling against Enghien it is not found in the official record. There he is reported only as saying what he had already told Dautancourt, that he had served in the *Armée de Condé* and that he hoped to see service in the new war between England and France.

He was asked if he had any more to say. He repeated his request for an interview with the First Consul. This was the end of the trial. He was taken back to his room, the hall was cleared, and the judges sat down to deliberate.

They knew what they were expected to do and they did it. They knew just enough law to concoct a document which was sufficiently crammed with overloaded grammar and jargon to look legal to an uninstructed eye. It recorded a unanimous verdict that Enghien was guilty and was therefore condemned to death—*condamné à la peine de mort*. They informed Savary. They knew that they were doing evil and at the last minute, perhaps suddenly realizing their ignominy after pronouncing their verdict, they decided to make one last vain effort to save their own consciences and possibly put matters right.

The Duke of Enghien had several times asked for a personal

interview with the First Consul and had put this down in writing. There was nothing in their instructions which forbade them to support such a request, daring as their action might be. Hulin recorded the next episode:

'Hardly had the judgement been signed than I sat down to write a letter in which, with the unanimous agreement of the Commission, I informed the First Consul of the wish, as we had heard it expressed several times by the Prince, that he might have an interview with him. I also urged the First Consul to remit a sentence which on account of our rigorous instructions could not be avoided in our judgement.

'At that moment a man who had remained in the hall throughout came up to me.

' "What are you doing there?" he asked.

'I replied "I am writing to the First Consul in order to acquaint him with our wishes and those of the condemned man."

'He took the pen from my hand. "Your task is finished" the man said, "the rest is my business. [*Maintenant çela me regarde*]." '

Hulin raised no further resistance. Nor did any of his colleagues. 'The man', needless to say, was Savary. Needless to say, also, the letter was never sent. Needless to say, as well, when Napoleon heard about the incident he made some excellent propaganda out of it, and said that had he known he would have grasped the opportunity to pardon this fine young man, and would like to have made him a general in the French army. It is more than unlikely that there is a word of truth in any of this. According to one of Napoleon's versions the letter was intercepted by Talleyrand, but Talleyrand was nowhere near Vincennes. The only place he is reported to have been in the early morning of 'the 30th of Ventôse' was the drawing-room of the Vicomtesse de Laval where he was observed to pull out his watch from time to time.

Before being informed of the verdict and sentence, indeed before the trial had even begun, Savary had arranged for a firing-party of sixteen men to get ready. One of them described what happened after they had been marched down into the moat beneath the Pavillion de la Reine: 'At the end of a half-hour of silence and standing which seemed much longer we were told that there was a conspirator who had been very rightly condemned to death because he wanted to overturn everything and put France back into the horrors of the last days of Robespierre. We were told he would be brought out soon and put opposite us at four or five paces and that the signal to fire would be given by an officer facing the criminal, and that the signal would be first, to put his hand to his cap and then, for the firing, to take off his cap. We said it was so dark that we could not see but they said they were looking after that.'

The Duke of Enghien was in his room talking to a young officer called Noirot of the *gendarmerie d'élite*. He asked him about modern army life in France, and what service he had seen. While they were chatting together there was a bang on the door and Harel and Brigadier-Sergeant Aufort came in, the Sergeant bearing a large lighted lantern. Harel requested the prisoner to come with him. Enghien took up his hat and followed the two men, with Noirot and several gendarmes. They went down into the main courtyard and across to a door in one of the towers. It was cold and raining. Suddenly, as they entered the tower door, Enghien was overcome with horror. 'Where are you taking me?' he cried to Harel.

There was no answer.

'Are you taking me to the dungeons?' he asked. 'I would as soon die!'

Again there was silence. Then one of the gendarmes said, 'No, not to the dungeons . . . unfortunately.'

Harel then spoke those traditional words which can have only one meaning. 'Monsieur,' he said, 'please follow me and summon all your courage.'

Enghien immediately understood. They walked in silence through the tower, across the drawbridge, down a wooden staircase into the moat, and soon found themselves face to face with the firing-party. An officer was there with a lantern. When in the dim light he had ascertained who was who in the party he set down the lantern, drew a document from the inner pocket of his overcoat, and read out the judgement, verdict, and sentence.

When he had come to the end of this rigmarole Enghien turned to Lieutenant Noirot and asked him if he would do him a last service. Noirot said he would. He then asked for some scissors. All the men in the firing-party began hunting in their pockets and cartridge pouches for scissors, and eventually a pair was found. It was handed to him and he cut off a lock of his hair. He wrapped it with his wedding ring in a letter which he had written and said to Noirot, 'Send this to Princess Charlotte de Rohan-Rochefort in Ettenheim.' Noirot said he would. He tried to be faithful to his promise but was prevented by the authorities. The packet went to Réal, who did not send it on.

Enghien asked the officer in charge of the firing-party, a man called Adjutant Pelé, if he could have a priest. Standing in the moat near the wall of the castle the voices carried. When he had asked for a priest a man leaning out of a window high up in the wall shouted: 'What! Does he want to die like a monk? [*Veut-il donc mourir en capucin?*]' It was too dark to see who he was, but several witnesses said later that the man was Savary. One cannot be sure. He was such a horrible man that people sometimes imagined him worse than he was. Yet it is certain that someone jeered in those stupid words at the wretched man facing death.

He looked up indignantly, then asked the officer again. No, said Pelé, it was impossible. There was no chaplain in the castle. There was not time to fetch a priest from outside. He was sorry. Enghien went on his knees, made the sign of the cross, and prayed for a short time. He then rose and cried out, '*Qu'il est affreux de périr ainsi de la main des français.*'

Adjutant Pelé put his hand to his cap, which he immediately

pulled off. The party fired and the Duke of Enghien fell forward dead.

They took off his long coat and his hunting cap and emptied his pockets. When they had divided the spoils they carried the body to the grave nearby, threw it in face-downwards, and quickly toiled with spades to cover it in with earth. Howls and wails were heard within the castle and presently scampering steps which rushed over the drawbridge and down the wooden staircase into the moat. It was the pug-dog Mohiloff. Whining and crying he scratched and dug into the earth which covered his master's body. He was the only mourner.

The soldiers chased Mohiloff away and he vanished for the time being, but on the next day he came back to the grave several times until a kindly man who lived in the town of Vincennes, and who was employed in the fortress, took him back to his house. Thereafter for the rest of his life Mohiloff lived in what Henri Welschinger rightly describes as '*un asile mérité.*'

Soon after the execution and the burial Savary collected the men of the *gendarmerie d'élite* and the Paris garrison to lead them back. The speed with which they had been assembled and sent to Vincennes allows one to suppose that the troops were all mounted. One must imagine a cavalcade of about a hundred and twenty men in the strange and often grotesque military uniforms of the early nineteenth century (uniforms whose style is preserved in the French Garde Republicaine and the British Life Guards and Horse Guards) jingling back to Paris at a slow trot towards five in the morning of a raw March day with the dawn coming up. All soldiers, even the worst, detest execution business. Considerable efforts had been made to denigrate the man they had executed during the preceding night, but there is evidence that some hours before the hateful act everyone at Vincennes, both troops and permanent staff, knew who the prisoner was. One should never forget the odd telepathic knowledge of affairs that exists in any army. It is not too fanciful, on that account, to suppose that the journey back to Paris from Vincennes, like the journey from Ettenheim to Strasbourg, was undertaken in a state of gloom.

Savary bore the official documents relating to the execution, documents, be it noted by all lawyers, that were many times more numerous than the documentation on which the trial had been instituted. The key document was from Major Harel to Councillor of State Réal and read as follows:

'Citizen Councillor, I have the honour to inform you that the individual who arrived on the 29th instant [the 29th Ventôse=the 20th March] at the castle of Vincennes at five and a half hours of the afternoon was, in the course of the ensuing night, judged by a military commission and shot at three in the morning, and buried within the confines of the place of which I have the honour to be the Commandant. I have the honour to salute you with the deepest respect. Harel.'

To the sinister drama of the returning cavalcade Réal tried desperately to add another. Like so many who later struggled to free themselves from the responsibilities of March 21st, 1804, Réal invented stories about himself. There is no doubt that Napoleon sent him detailed instructions for the interrogation of Enghien, but there is also no doubt that the questions in that document were no more than a slightly elaborated version of the questions put to Enghien by Dautancourt. The case put forward by Réal is that he was given the full authority of the First Consul to judge the guilt of the prisoner and to pronounce sentence; that the instructions from Malmaison did not reach his house till ten o'clock of the evening of the 20th of March and—this is the most absurd part of the story, considering the abject fear of the First Consul which afflicted everyone concerned—that his staff did not like to wake him up as he had gone to bed early after a more than usually fatiguing day. The result, he said, was that he was not told of his mission till three in the morning, the moment of the execution. From these imaginings Réal concocted a pathetic story that at the same time as Savary led his cavalcade back to

Paris, he, Réal, was travelling in his carriage to Vincennes on his mission of government service and mercy. The story then goes on that he and Savary met, whereupon Réal learned with amazement and grief that the young prisoner had already been condemned and shot.

There is no reason to believe a word of Réal's story. The only grain of truth that it contains is to be found in what occurred the day before, when Maret saw General Murat. What certainly did happen on the 21st was that Savary, presumably calling at his house, informed Réal of the death of the Duke of Enghien, and that they both then went separately to La Malmaison. Savary arrived first. He began to give Napoleon a detailed account of the events of the night, when Réal arrived. Napoleon, according to the account of his secretary Méneval, interrupted to ask Réal why he also had not been present at Vincennes. 'After listening to his explanations,' says Méneval, without mentioning the supposed slumbers or the dawn meeting on the road to Paris, 'and after exchanging a few remarks with him, the First Consul fell once more into a mood of silent abstraction. Then without letting fall a word of censure or commendation he took up his hat and said, '*C'est bien!*' leaving Monsieur Réal in a state of surprise and some preoccupation.' One can imagine what Napoleon's reaction would have been if Réal had really been charged with a mission to reprieve Enghien, and had failed to carry it out through oversleeping.

There was no one of the principals concerned in the murder of the Duke of Enghien who did not try in after years to prove his innocence. With one exception they all failed. The most interesting case is that of Napoleon. Loss of life was not a matter which bothered him much. 'What are a million men to me!' he is reported to have said on one occasion, and it must certainly be put to his credit that he gave a worthy example, facing death, whenever he did, with the utmost fortitude. Yet the murder of Enghien haunted him to the end. He was for ever bringing the hideous subject up during his years of power and of ruin. To take one example of many: On the eve of his departure for the Congress of Erfurt he proposed to Monsieur de Rémusat, at that time responsible for the administration of the Comédie Française, that the company should entertain the assembled sovereigns with a performance of Corneille's *Cinna*. He particularly wanted the sovereigns to hear the lines in which it is said that all 'crimes of the state' done on behalf of the Crown must ultimately receive divine sanction.

'Get a volume of Corneille,' said Napoleon.

'I know the lines,' said Monsieur de Rémusat, and recited:

> '*Tous ces crimes d'état qu'on fait pour la couronne*
> *Le Ciel nous en absout alors qu'il nous les donne,*
> *Et dans le sacré rang ou sa faveur l'a mis,*
> *Le passé devient juste et l'avenir permis,*
> *Qui peut y parvenir ne peut être coupable*
> *Quoi qu'il ait fait ou fasse, il est inviolable!*'

'That's excellent,' said Napoleon, 'and above all for these Germans who are always stuck with the same ideas and still talk about the death of the Duke of Enghien. We must enlarge their moral sense.'

Yet the same man held it against Talleyrand that he had drawn him into this atrocity, a very unjust though not quite baseless accusation, and maintained the fiction that if he had been 'allowed' to meet Enghien the result would have been chivalrous, merciful, and beneficial to his country. In the memoirs he blamed the English government for promoting conspiracies and 'those who, driven on by a criminal zeal, did not wait for the orders of their sovereign before executing the judgement of the military commission', yet within a short time of dictating that version he wrote in his will that the murder was a necessary act of national 'security and interest' and added: 'In similar circumstances I would act in the same way.' It is surely manifest that he contradicted himself because he was haunted. Las Cases said in the *Memorial of St. Helena*,

'The Emperor often discussed this subject, and this helped me to observe many of his most pronounced and personal characteristics in all their subtlety.' Once he told Las Cases the real truth: 'Blood will have blood! Such is the way of nature, inevitable, infallible! Woe to him that provokes it!' When Napoleon speaks as a Corsican he can usually be believed.

The attempts of Murat, or rather of his friends, and of Réal, of Hulin, of Savary, and the rest to prove their innocence came to nothing in the light of history, though they all succeeded in saving their reputations for a time. Their stories were accepted during their time of life but were found out after. The exception is Talleyrand.

Like Napoleon he is the subject of a cult and on the whole a much more successful one. In spite of the accumulation of utterly damning evidence, chiefly the work of Henri Welschinger, the readers of the *Encyclopaedia Britannica* are to this day advised not to regard Talleyrand as guilty of any part of the greatest crime of his life. One can see why the cult succeeds. It appeals to more refined feelings than does the cult to which it stands in obvious rivalry. The cult of Napoleon is of a man of the utmost directness, even in his tergiversations, so that even when he lied he did so with a kind of direct shamelessness. The cult of Talleyrand is of a man who prided himself on skill in manœuvre, who loved to be an enigma, who remains fascinating because he set a question mark over himself and his time. So long as one looks at him superficially he can entrance one.

Unlike Napoleon, Talleyrand seems to have had no promptings of remorse until it was a matter of vital self-interest that he dissociate himself from Napoleon's deed. Before then he took some pride in looking at the thing with aristocratic cynicism. Less emotional than Napoleon, he could defend the atrocity with a wit that was so keen that it makes one laugh today. Shortly after March 1804 the Russian Emperor Alexander I demanded to know why no enquiry had been made into the trial and execution of Enghien, and why no one had been punished for it. Talleyrand—not, one may suppose, disguising under his habitual politeness that he was aware that Alexander had played a far from innocent part in his own accession—replied that when the Russian Emperor's august predecessor Tsar Paul I had been murdered in 1801, in St. Petersburg, no one, so far as he knew, had been punished for the crime, and the Consular French Government, in which he had had the honour to serve as Minister for External Relations, had not felt it their duty to intervene in that deplorable affair. . . . Alexander changed the topic.

None of this, nor of his desperate attempts to clear himself in public, in 1823, when Savary tried to throw the blame from himself on to Talleyrand, really tells us what was in Talleyrand's mind. He claimed in his memoirs that such an act as that of March 21st was out of keeping with his character and his record. There was something in this line of defence. There was no streak of cruelty in Talleyrand as there undoubtedly was in Napoleon. But there was the same streak of inhumanity. He had to choose between consent to a murder and danger to a great career. He did not hesitate for a second.

He loved his country. To get France out of the disastrous cycle of wars into which the genius of Napoleon led her, Talleyrand was prepared to cheat and swindle and lie and betray without limit, always on the understanding that the France he saved was a France with Talleyrand at the top. That was as far as his moral sense could go. No one can deny that it included real patriotism. It is probably true to say that he saved France in 1814. It is also true to say that two years later, when he had lost office, he toyed with the idea of betraying both the throne and the liberalism for which he had fought in 1814. He was big enough on occasion to see things in a detached way, but he was always incurably and revoltingly selfish.

He shocked his contemporaries, yet they found that in spite of themselves they could not resist him. Napoleon had magnetism which either bound men to him or repelled them. Talleyrand had charm, and the charm turned out to be a

longer-term investment than Napoleon's magnetism. It did him
good service when he was alive, and kept his reputation after
his death. His excuses (unlike Napoleon's) for murdering the
Duke of Enghien have been accepted by many people who
find it hard to resist the cult of so witty, genial, interesting,
and occasionally wise a man. To think of him as a murderer
seems an affront to taste. And why think of him as a murderer
when there is a much likely culprit staring one imperially in
the face, who said he would do the same again, and who, when
told of the horrible details, could think of nothing else to say
than '*C'est bien!*' But Talleyrand was a murderer too, just as
much as Napoleon.

Apart from his declarations of innocence, in which in old
age he may have come to believe, he did not, as noted already,
allow men to see what was in his mind regarding this dark
episode. But even the most crafty and disciplined of men can
be taken by surprise. This happened to Talleyrand on the
morning of March 21st. He came to his Ministry, late as
usual, and perhaps especially late after his night of card-
playing at Madame de Laval's. One of his senior subordinates,
a man called Monsieur d'Hauterive, who was head of a
department 'dealing with the London, Vienna, Berlin, and
Amsterdam correspondence', came to him with an ashen face.
Talleyrand asked him what was the matter. But, cried Hauterive,
'*avec sa grosse voix*', had not the Citizen Minister read *Le
Moniteur* of that morning? *Le Moniteur*—what was so special
in *Le Moniteur*? But, exclaimed Hauterive, with gestures (we
are told by a witness) expressing disgust and rage, there is an
official communication announcing the resolution of a military
commission that the Duke of Enghien—the Ettenheim man—
the man who was brought into the courtyard in a coach yesterday—but yesterday—less than twenty-four hours ago—was
found guilty of conspiracy and that he had been condemned
a la peine de mort—and—without delay—he had been there
and then shot! This morning. At Vincennes. Not a rumour.
An official announcement! How, Hauterive asked in a passion,

could he, how could the Citizen Minister, how could any man
of honour continue to serve a government that was capable of
such an absolute negation of law and decency and civilization?

The announcement in *Le Moniteur* was certainly much sooner
than expected—perhaps another part of Savary's hideous insistence throughout on speed. It was now Talleyrand's duty to
say the right thing to set his subordinate's mind at rest. But
he had been taken unawares. He paused till he found something to say. And what did Talleyrand find in his soul to say?
His answer was so fantastic and so ordinary at the same time
that one almost forgets to hate the man who gave it. '*Eh bien,
quoi!*' Talleyrand replied. '*Ce sont les affaires.*' And that, if
you look at the evidence, is all that he ever seriously thought
about it.

A few people came out of the business with honour. When
the First Consul first ordained a trial of Enghien, when he
believed that he was guilty, and wanted a show-piece before a
public miltary tribunal, Murat asked a certain Colonel Préval
to sit as a member and assist in the composition of the body.
Préval replied that as both he and his father had in past times
served in the Enghien Regiment he could not comply with the
request. Every detail of the matter was under the First Consul's
eye, and this was known. Préval's action was more courageous
than may appear from a bare recital of the facts. From a
relatively humble position he was protesting against the breach
of law in the invasion of Baden. It was all the more courageous
in that he had every reason to suppose that Enghien was guilty.

The name of Chateaubriand must always be admiringly
remembered in this connection. Chateaubriand himself set
the good example and fairly lavished praise on himself. On
the morning of March 21st he too bought a copy of *Le Moniteur*.
He also read the news from Vincennes. 'That sentence', he
recorded later, 'changed the whole course of my life, as it did
Napoleon's.' At that time Chateaubriand, still well thought of
by the government for his *Le Génie du Christianisme* which, it
was said, had made the Consular Concordat possible, was a

member of the staff of the Foreign Ministry, and under orders
to report to Rome as an attaché to the French Embassy. He
immediately wrote to his chief:

'Citizen Minister, The doctors have just informed me that the
state of Madame de Chateaubriand's health is such as to arouse
fears for her life. As, in the circumstances, it is utterly impossible that I should either leave my wife or expose her to the
risks of a journey, I beg that Your Excellency will permit me
to return the letters of credit and instructions.'

Men believed that the reign of Terror had reopened.
This was a brave thing to do, and the example was not
followed.

The man who comes out with most credit, because he showed
courage and consistency throughout, is Monsieur Massias. It
was he who, quite unwittingly and more than anyone else,
showed up Talleyrand as a hollow man and makes nonsense
of the cult. He did everything he could to prevent the crime, but
to accomplish this end he acted on the assumption that there
was a particle of honesty in his chief. He seriously miscalcula-
ted. When it was over, Talleyrand wrote to him telling him that
the First Consul was under the impression that Madame
Massias was related to Madame de Reich, and would Monsieur
Massias kindly tell him the facts of the case. He did not
mention, of course, that it was he, Talleyrand, and only he,
who had impressed the fable on the First Consul. It is difficult
to see why Talleyrand wrote the letter—perhaps he was
ordered to, or perhaps he thought that there was just a hope
in a thousand that the ladies *were* related; you never know
your luck, and he had a weakness for gambling. Monsieur
Massias wrote back from Carlsruhe that his wife was in no
way related to or connected with Madame de Reich. Pity.
Needless to say, Talleyrand did not show the answer to the
First Consul.

In the early summer of that year, after Napoleon had been
declared French Emperor, Massias was ordered to go to Aix la
Chapelle to pay his respects. Marshal Lannes warned him that

the Emperor was very angry with him because he regarded him as a crypto-royalist. He was shown into Napoleon's study where he found him with Talleyrand and a secretary.

'Now then, Monsieur Massias,' said the Emperor, 'how does it come about that though I have treated you with the utmost generosity, you have not scrupled to enter into the miserable intrigues of the enemies of France?'

Massias looked from one to the other in amazement.

'Well, really,' said the Emperor, 'one would suppose that the man didn't know what I was talking about.'

Massias indicated that this was the case.

'*Comment?*' exclaimed the Emperor. 'Is it not the fact that you are married to a close relative of a miserable intriguer, the Baronne de Reich? What do you say to that?'

Massias there and then saw through Talleyrand. He turned on his betrayer and spoke as follows:

'Sire, that man at your side has most unworthily abused the good faith of Your Majesty. He knows from me that my wife is no relation whatever of Madame de Reich, and to prove it I have even sent him an official certificate of her origins.'

The Emperor was momentarily pacified and in a milder tone asked him, 'None the less you have allowed meetings of emigrants to take place at Offenburg, haven't you?'

Massias replied: 'I have given reliable accounts, sire, of everything of note which has happened in the area of my legation. How could I with any justice be expected to persecute a few wretched people at the same time as under your administration people of this kind, emigrants, were and still are being allowed to cross the Rhine back into France by hundreds and thousands? It was my endeavour to act in accordance with the spirit of your government.'

The Emperor then said, 'All the same, you should have prevented the Duke of Enghien from hatching his plots at Ettenheim.'

Massias replied: 'Sire, I am too advanced in years to learn how to lie. Once again the good faith of Your Majesty has been abused as regards that matter. [*On a encore trompé sur ce point la religion de Votre Majesté*].'

Talleyrand got the Emperor back where he wanted him, and next day Monsieur Massias was the object of Napoleon's studied discourtesy in public, but in the end his career suffered no disadvantage. He became Consul General in Danzig and then Intendant. He was made a Baron of the Empire. Here one should mention that though Napoleon loaded his accomplices and accessaries with rewards after the crime, he did not wreak his vengeance against the few people who gave honour to their country by standing out against tyranny. Préval suffered no disadvantage, nor did Chateaubriand on this account, nor did his brother Joseph, nor in the end did Massias. There was not much generosity in Napoleon, but, when it was not too inconvenient to do so, he respected courage.

The murder was successful in the sense that the primary objectives were attained. There was an immediate decline in royalist conspiracy and royalism itself was not an important factor in the history of the Empire till its last months. People at the time considered that the crime led to the foundation of the Empire. This is probably a confusion with the fact that the need to crush the reviving royalism in the country certainly gave added reason to the Imperial party to hurry on their plans. Cadoudal said at his trial, 'We came to give France a king, but instead we have given her an emperor.' This was true, but there is no reason to suppose that the Empire needed a murderous human sacrifice at its initiation. In the long term the crime was as stupid as it was wicked. The only person who did well out of it was Fouché. As a result of the crime he got his Ministry of Police without being grossly involved in its guilt. It also added to his reputation as a wit. He made the most famous remark about the murder. '*C'est plus qu'un crime*,' he said, '*c'est une faute.*'

The blunder brought to an end an era of hope and honour. It destroyed the image, as we would say nowadays, of Napoleon. The whole splendour of the man during the days of the Consulate was that he came as a breath of fresh air, that he undertook the role of the reconciler of new and ancient, and that such was the power of his genius that he could live up to this enormous promise. The conception of Napoleon as the embodiment of Roman Republican virtue in modern guise was destroyed beyond repair by this act of spite and meanness and mercilessness. Beethoven's famous exclamation, 'Then he is only an ordinary man after all!' applies with devastating force here. Rémusat obviously exaggerated absurdly when he went so far as to say that Napoleon launched into the wars of the Empire to cover up the shame of March 1804, but the exaggeration is of a truth. He could never be trusted again in the same way. Henceforth he ruled by might and less and less, and soon not at all, by moral force. Power corrupted him earlier than most men. This was the first sign that the malady had gone far.

How would the Enghien case go today? We cannot look back to 1804 with any sense of moral superiority. Our century is not an innocent one in the matter of judicial murder: the trial was accurately prophetic of Nazi and Communist legal procedures. But this is to refer to systems of rule which reject the European civilization to which Consular France belonged. What of the countries which still hold to that way of life? The Eichmann abduction was similar to Enghien's and was condoned. It is fairly safe to say that in a civilized court of law today the proof that Enghien was innocent of the conspiracy of which he was suspected would ensure that he would not suffer capital punishment, but it is doubtful whether we would on that account acquit him. Though innocent of the main charge, the young man, as the centre of a modern treason trial, would probably continue to appear as purely sinister to twentieth-century judges. No matter how skilfully it was defended in court, his behaviour would shock people today as indisputably treasonable.

The men who carried out the deed and the man who suffered all had old-fashioned ideas. They all venerated the name of the

Grand Condé through habit. He had been much more guilty of what Enghien was accused of than his unfortunate descendant, but he had had the luck to live before the age of nationalism. Enghien's defence, that he would fight against his country according to the rules of war, but not by underhand methods, would make little impression on public opinion in our time. It made an enormous impression then. That alone illustrates how much the men of that time still belonged to a former one. Here was Napoleon's mistake. He looked forward too early to the future which he was bringing to birth. He once said of himself, '*Je ne suis pas un homme mais une chose.*' In March 1804 he was true to this terrible intuition. That is the ultimate interest of this crime.

One other person should be remembered, Princess Charlotte de Rohan-Rochefort. On March 16th she followed her husband to Strasbourg. She did not see him. She was interrogated by the Prefect and sent back to Ettenheim. Lamartine has a story that she arrived at Vincennes shortly after the execution. He is a fascinating authority, an invaluable source of contemporary evidence for the period, but on this occasion he seems to have too completely surrendered to his weakness: if a story was sufficiently romantic, then, in the eyes of this otherwise admirable witness, it was nine-tenths true. In fact she went back to Ettenheim.

She lived two years in her former home, and then went to Hungary with her father, who was accorded a pension by Alexander I. She never returned to Ettenheim after 1806 and we hear of her in different places in the German-speaking world during the next eight years: Vienna, Pressburg, Munich. One effect of the disaster may have been to make her restless, and in a letter of 1814 she says she feels condemned to a life of wandering.

In 1815 Louis XVIII offered to acknowledge her officially as Duchess of Enghien. She replied as follows:

'Since Your Majesty was opposed to such a declaration in the days when the Duke of Enghien was alive, and when to bear that name would have given me the utmost joy, now that I can only bear it in the sorrow of mourning I would prefer that nothing is done.'

She gave her mind to religious exercise. One of her best friends was Princess Louise de Condé, the Duke of Bourbon's sister, who had entered a religious order under the name of Sister Marie-Joséph de la Miséricorde. This remarkable woman deeply loved her nephew Enghien, but after his murder, so she told in a letter to a clergyman, she prayed for Napoleon every day at Mass. She could not influence Princess Charlotte to imitate her noble form of piety. To the end the widow loathed Napoleon with the whole of her being. She remained embittered, though very much an object of affection. In her later years she lived permanently in Paris. Her house was in the Rue de Lille and there she died in 1841.